Cape Cod Harvest

Harvest

A Gathering in of Cape Cod Stories

Cape Cod Harvest

A Gathering in of Cape Cod Stories

By Jim Coogan & Jack Sheedy

Harvest Home Books
East Dennis, Massachusetts

Cape Cod Harvest

First Printing – March 2007

Published by
Harvest Home Books,
P.O. Box 1181
East Dennis, Massachusetts 02641

ISBN 0-9672596-6-5
ISBN 978-0-9672596-6-6

Cover design and text layout by
Jackie Rockwell of Rockwell Design

Printed in the United States of America

Additional copies of Cape Cod Harvest
and the authors' previous books
(Cape Cod Companion & Cape Cod Voyage)
may be obtained by contacting
Harvest Home Books at the address above.

www.harvesthomebooks.com

Contents

Introduction

This is not necessarily a Cape Cod history book. And we have not titled it as such.

True, the stories are rooted in local history. But rather than just annotated facts wrapped in a general chronology, what we have selected are more the interpretations of events as seen through the eyes of people who have lived here. In much the same way that our ancient ancestors gathered around campfires to hear elders detail tribal history, so are these stories a reflection of tales told and retold by generations of Cape Codders.

Many of these tales are factual accounts from familiar sources. Some are more anecdotal and difficult to substantiate. We've culled them from a variety of places—old newspapers, obscure and out of print books, genealogies, and personal interviews. We'll admit to even picking up a few at some local drinking establishments!

Most are not from primary sources and many admittedly skirt the edges of legend. But, like a piece of fabric, the wrap of folklore mixes with the weft of fact to make the whole cloth. Both strands contribute to a sense of what a place really is—or in this case, what it was. We'll be glad to leave the sorting out to historians and hope that you enjoy the "harvest" of our efforts.

Jim Coogan
March, 2007
Sandwich, Massachusetts

Foreword

According to Webster, the definition of the word "harvest" is "to gather in, to reap." In that sense, this third collaborative effort—the follow-up to our earlier *Cape Cod Companion* and *Cape Cod Voyage*—is truly a gathering in of various tales from Cape Cod's past. Some of the tales in *Cape Cod Harvest* may sound familiar; many of them may not. Yet together, these tales form a bountiful harvest reaped from various libraries and historical societies, from countless books and journals, and from more intangible elements such as hearsay and rumor. The result is a combination of history and lore, with blurred lines separating the two.

In all cases, we focus on the tale, of course with a watchful eye on the facts. Yet, it is the tale embedded within the history that makes these stories worth repeating. As the years unfurl, these tales from the Cape's past grow more and more golden. Now even the 20th century seems a bygone era, after all, it is clearly last century. And because of that fact, we include two full chapters of tales from that past century.

Like Chaucer's *Canterbury Tales*, our three "Cape Cod" volumes, culminating in the volume you hold in your hands, is a swapping of stories between friends. From *Companion* to *Voyage* to *Harvest*, we have attempted to bring together salty tales of this wonderful peninsula for the enjoyment of our readers. Truth be told, we, too, have enjoyed these stories ... or rather we have enjoyed the pursuit of them. There is a sense of personal satisfaction in tracking down a good story, and then serving it up for others to read and muse over. One could say, as writing companions we have enjoyed the voyage that has led to this latest harvest of tales.

Finally, as you read these tales remember that the characters involved were people just like all of us. In many cases they were simple people who somehow managed to do amazing things. Yet, it was this simple nature that made their feats all that more impressive.

Jack Sheedy
March, 2007
Dennis, Massachusetts

Chapter 1

The Coming of the Pilgrims

Begin any story about Cape Cod's past and you find yourself back in the time of Native Americans and Mayflower Pilgrims. From Native tales of creation to Pilgrim tales of perseverance, it forms a first chapter in our shared local history.

Maushop and Granny Squannit

Though geologists claim that a half-mile high glacier pushed its way south from northern lands, thus creating the peninsula of Cape Cod, the Natives of the area had a much different explanation of how the landmass was formed.

It was their belief that the Great Spirit Kehtean created the lands and the waters that we see today, as well as the skies that stretch above the two. Further, they believed that a local giant named Maushop created the islands of Nantucket and Martha's Vineyard with sands which he dumped from his moccasins. He is also credited with creating the fog so prevalent in the area with smoke from his pipe.

In Dennis, Maushop made Scargo Lake and Scargo Hill, as well as the pine trees encircling the lake and dotting the hill, which sprouted from the ashes of his pipe. Smoke from his pipe created thunderclouds that produced days of rain—enough rainwater, in fact, to fill the lake. Of course, geologists have their own explanation that involves a receding glacier and a large cake of melting ice that formed a water-filled hollow in the sandy terrain.

Maushop's wife, Quaunt, had five giant sons who took after their father, yet the Pukwudgees, a band of "Little People," set upon the sons and killed them with their magical powers. The five were buried in the waters off Woods Hole, their graves covered with sand to produce what we today call the Elizabeth Islands. Again, geologists point to their glacier theory.

There is another being of which the Natives spoke that played a role in their daily lives, and perhaps plays a role on Cape Cod even today. Granny Squannit, or Tooquahmisquannit in the Native tongue, is said to have lived along the northern Cape in a dune cave, somewhere near the great marshes. She possessed singular physical features—she was short in stature with webbed fingers and long hair that concealed her face. One of her feet was larger than the other, thus creating strange footprints in the sands along the beaches. Yet her most distinguishing feature was a single eye in the very center of her forehead.

Granny Squannit used local herbs to make secret magic potions and was thus able to communicate with animals. Envious of Maushop's special powers, she once bargained with a whale to steal the giant's pipe, promising one thousand trout in payment. The slick whale had different ideas, and stole the pipe for himself. But that didn't stop Granny Squannit; she tricked the leviathan, luring it close to shore. When he was close enough, she caused the tide to go out, thus beaching the whale. Perhaps she has something to do with the occasional beaching of whales and dolphins that still occurs today.

Natives of the Cape celebrated a special day in honor of Granny Squannit marked with offerings of food and ceremonial dances. She was especially associated with the native cranberry, which the Wampanoags called sassamanesh. Eaten raw or cooked in a sauce, sassamanesh was sometimes mixed with venison to create pemmican, a protein-rich food. The Natives believed the berries were a gift from their Great Spirit, delivered by a dove, and cared for by Granny Squannit to assure a bountiful harvest. At harvest time it was customary to offer up a basket of the berries, which would be left at the marsh for Squannit.

Besides cranberries, it seems that Granny Squannit was also fond of treasures, particularly gold, and used glowing orbs to mark the location of her buried treasures. Natives knew never to dig beneath an orb for fear of angering her. It is interesting to note that throughout different periods of Cape Cod history there have been tales of such glowing orbs. One can only imagine the riches marked by each of these mysterious globes!

Cape Cod's Columbus

The year 2002 marked the 400th anniversary of a significant event in Cape Cod history, one that saw the first English explorer step foot upon these shores. In fact, an event that led to the naming of this place for its plentiful codfish.

English explorer Bartholomew Gosnold was nothing less than Cape Cod's Christopher Columbus. Born in 1571 into an influential family at Suffolk, England—one of nine children—he was the son of Anthony Gosnold, a lawyer, and Dorothy Bacon, whose ancestry included Francis Bacon. Family connections and wealth would help Gosnold later when he applied for patents to explore the New World.

While away at college Gosnold became interested in tales of voyages and attended lectures and read texts on the subject. His later marriage to Mary Golding, the daughter of a lawyer and granddaughter of London's Lord Mayor, helped to introduce Gosnold to many influential people. In a major career move, Gosnold became a successful privateer who sacked a number of Spanish vessels and ports during Britain's war with Spain. Gosnold's successes had gained him a favorable reputation. When Queen Elizabeth offered patents to open up trade routes to the East Indies, Gosnold's connections helped him to become chosen as captain of the bark *Concord* with a mission to build a trading post in the New World. He and his crew were also to search for valuable resources, document the flora and fauna, test the soils, and determine whether a permanent settlement could be established.

Leaving Falmouth, England in April 1602, the Atlantic crossing was relatively uneventful, though it is believed that Gosnold discovered the Gulf Stream. The vessel reached the coast of Maine by mid-May and within days Gosnold and his men encountered Natives. During a friendly meeting on board the *Concord*, one of the Natives drew a map of the coastline on the deck of the ship, a map showing the outline of Cape Cod!

Gosnold sailed south to the tip of the Cape, anchoring at Provincetown Harbor. There he and some of his men went ashore, becoming the first Englishmen to set foot in New England. At

Provincetown the crew caught a number of codfish, prompting Gosnold to rename the landmass from Shoal Hope (his first choice) to Cape Cod.

Gosnold continued south around Monomoy and into Nantucket Sound, following the coastline until he reached an island where he went ashore. The explorer named this island—so rich in grape vines—for his deceased daughter, Martha.

After leaving Martha's Vineyard, he explored a chain of islands nearby, and one in particular that appeared to be an ideal spot to set up a trading post. He called it Elizabeth Island (now Cuttyhunk Island, as the entire chain is now known as the Elizabeth Islands). On that island Gosnold had the men construct their encampment.

One spring day some Natives paddled from the peninsula out to the island and stayed for a few days. The thirty or so Englishmen dined with more than fifty Indians in a Thanksgiving-type affair. Gosnold wrote in a letter to his father of the Natives' disposition: "The inhabitants there ... being of tall stature, comely proportion, strong, active, and some of good years, and as it should seem very healthful, are sufficient proof of the healthfulness of the place."

Although the original plan was to establish a permanent settlement, with a number of men staying behind while the *Concord* sailed for England to collect more men and fresh supplies, the crew decided against it, perhaps due to low provisions and threat of Indian attack. After just one month in the New World, the *Concord* set sail, arriving back at England by late July.

Although Gosnold never returned to Cape Cod, he was a key participant in the settlement of Jamestown, Virginia in 1607, commanding one of the expedition's three ships—the *God Speed*. Like a number of the settlers, he died of illness during the first year and was buried in the soil of the New World.

A Dark Pilgrim Tale
Combining unrequited love, a strange twist of fate, and maybe even suicide will produce a story line that could fill the themes of daytime television. Add an unhappy marriage, a move away from loved ones and familiar surroundings to a new and inhospitable

place, to the melancholy that might affect a person confronted by these situations, and you have a prescription for tragedy—the purest of plot themes.

All of these elements were present aboard the ship *Mayflower* as it lay at anchor in Provincetown Harbor in December of 1620. And they appear to have all come together to determine the fate of Dorothy Bradford, the first wife of the legendary governor of the Plymouth Colony.

Her death, which resulted from a fall overboard from the *Mayflower* in mid-December 1620, is a fact reported by history. In his recollection, *Of Plimoth Plantation*, William Bradford records the loss of his wife of seven years with a simple notation: "William Bradford his wife dyed soone after their arrivall." There is no mention of the circumstances and it was not until some time after the event that another writer let it be known that Dorothy Bradford drowned after falling overboard. Beyond that simple statement in Bradford's notes, there is nothing. What makes it more interesting is the fact that Bradford goes into considerable detail about the deaths of some of the other members of the Pilgrim party. Why so abrupt at the loss of his own wife? Looking deeper into the marriage

The Mayflower at anchor at Cape Cod, 1620. (Cape Cod Community College)

of Dorothy and William Bradford, the story becomes even more interesting—and curious.

As a young man, William Bradford was living with other members of the Separatist community in the Dutch city of Leyden. One of the families there was that of Alexander Carpenter. Of his five daughters, it is said that Alice caught young William's fancy and he ardently pursued her until he was advised by the father that she could never be his because he was just a poor weaver. Alice eventually married Edward Southworth whose ancestry was more noteworthy. Just six months later, William wed 16-year-old Dorothy May, a woman apparently more suitable for his lowly status in life. Whether he loved her or whether the marriage was simply a rebound reflex can never really be known. They had one child, a son, in seven years of marriage prior to 1620. Dorothy dutifully accompanied her husband across the Atlantic on the *Mayflower* that fall. The son was left behind in the care of other sect members.

If indeed William Bradford harbored continuing affection for his former love interest Alice Carpenter, Dorothy most certainly would have sensed it. And as a mother, she missed her only child. With an almost nightmarish scenario of suffering surrounding her, and doubts about the future in such a bleak wilderness playing out aboard the *Mayflower*, it's no stretch to see Dorothy Bradford as entering the throes of a deep depression. Did it cause her to take her own life? That is something that cannot be known. Her body was never recovered and there were apparently no witnesses to her drowning. But the fact that the *Mayflower* was at anchor in a calm harbor makes it difficult to see her death as a simple accident. The contemporary impulse to suspect the husband in some kind of foul play arrangement also doesn't work here. William Bradford was with the exploring party that had taken the *Mayflower's* small boat several days earlier to explore the outer Cape for a suitable site for settlement. He did not learn of his wife's death until he returned.

But the tale takes an interesting twist from this point and this is probably why rumors have continued to dog the story of Dorothy Bradford's death for more than three centuries. In the spring of 1621, the *Mayflower* returned to England. Aboard the ship was the list of those who had died during that first terrible winter.

Almost certainly, that list was conveyed to the Separatist members who had remained behind in England. Only three months earlier, Edward Southworth had died, leaving Alice Carpenter Southworth a widow. The *Mayflower* death list would have confirmed to her that she and her first love were now both without spouses. When the ship *Fortune* sailed for Plymouth in 1621, there was no doubt a letter from Alice addressed to the new Governor of the Plimoth Colony—William Bradford. There was no issue of his status now— nor of hers. More communication most certainly followed in 1622. A year later Alice was aboard the ship *Anne* bound for Plimoth. It would seem that this was more than just a mere coincidence. Just about a month after her arrival in the colony, in August of 1623, Alice Carpenter Southworth became the wife of William Bradford.

"Fell" From Grace

In November 1620, the *Mayflower* nearly came to woe on the rips and bars along the outer Cape. Captain Christopher Jones thought better of continuing on, and so he turned his vessel around and headed back to the Cape tip to anchor within the protection of Provincetown Harbor. Six years later, the captain and crew of the *Sparrowhawk* were not so wise, and as a result, not so lucky.

The 40-foot *Sparrowhawk* was bound for Virginia with some 25 people aboard, and a captain ill with scurvy. Though the vessel was woefully off course and onboard provisions were nearly exhaust- ed, a coastline suddenly appeared on the horizon. Unfamiliar with this shoreline, and unaware of the treacherous bars, *Sparrowhawk* and her crew became wrecked at Nauset Beach. All hands survived and made it to shore where they met Natives, some of whom spoke English. When news of the wreck made its way to Plimoth, and with it a request from the *Sparrowhawk* crew for assistance, William Bradford and others from the Plantation made the trip across the bay to Nauset Beach with materials to make repairs to the ship.

The crew was treated as guests of the Natives, as documented by Bradford in his journal: "They feasted these Indians and gave them many gifts." After repairs were made and the ship was deemed seaworthy, Bradford and the other Pilgrims made their way back to Plimoth after trading for corn with the local Natives. Yet the saga was not over. The *Sparrowhawk* was wrecked again "by the violence of a great storm and the bad mooring of their ship" according to Bradford. The crew once again appealed to Plimoth, this time asking if they might be put up "till they could have means to convey themselves to Virginia."

They spent the winter of 1626/27 at Plimoth, "sheltered in their houses as well as they could" wrote Bradford. "The chief amongst these people was one Mr. Fells and Mr. Sibsey, which had many servants belonging unto them, many of them being Irish."

After their winter stay at Plimoth, the former crew and passengers of the *Sparrowhawk* made their way to Virginia. There, Mr. Sibsey became a colony councilor. As for Mr. Fells, one could say he fell from grace. Apparently Fells had a maidservant at Plimoth whom, according to Bradford, "he was suspected to keep as his concubine." Fearing public ridicule and possible punishment for their behavior, the two quit Plimoth. Local folklore points to the naming of "Slut's Bush" at Nauset Beach as one of the sinful encampments frequented by Fells and his maidservant.

The Pilgrims' Trading Post
Commerce thrives off the practice of free trade. Healthy commerce grows the economy and fuels the engine that makes society work.

Aptucxet Trading Post. (Jack Sheedy photo)

Yet, trade can swiftly grind to a standstill without the ability to transport a product from the factory to the consumer. The *Mayflower* Pilgrims understood the importance of commerce and worked to develop avenues for easier trade with the Native Indians and other European settlers along the northeast coast. Such a trade system brought about the building of a trading post at old Sandwich (now Bourne) in 1627. This post was used to trade with the Dutch settlers at New Amsterdam—the Pilgrims trading furs in order to pay back the investors in England that originally funded the *Mayflower* expedition.

The trading post was strategically located to benefit from two rivers—the Scusset River from the north and the Manomet River from the south. These two waterways provided a largely water highway from Cape Cod Bay to Buzzards Bay, a route used by the Native Indians to cross the landmass via canoe with some portage in between. In fact, records show that the first boat built at Plimoth Colony, a pinnace, or small sailboat, was constructed at the trading post for use along the river.

In August 1635, a great hurricane caused much damage to the trading post and it was eventually abandoned. The march of the centuries and the wrath of the elements wiped out all traces of the original structure. Yet, its location was known to the locals, and a replica was built at the site in 1930. Known today as Aptucxet Trading Post, it is operated by the Bourne Historical Society and is open to the public.

Pilgrim Hopkins on Cape Cod

The courage of the *Mayflower* Pilgrims forms the first chapter in the settlement of Massachusetts and New England. They endured hardship and sacrifice, and many saw their dreams turn to disappointment. Although half their numbers died during the first winter, they somehow persevered. Theirs is the story of survival and ultimately, of success. Among these pioneers were legendary names such as Bradford, Standish, Brewster, Alden ... and Hopkins.

Born around 1578 in England, Stephen Hopkins was in his 40's when he, along with his second wife Elizabeth, and his three children, set off across the Atlantic. Elizabeth gave birth at sea, and the child was named Oceanus for its briny birthplace. As the *Mayflower* neared the coast of Cape Cod, it was Hopkins' daughter Constance who reportedly was the first to sight land.

A fact that is not well known is that Hopkins had previously visited America in 1609 when he sailed as a passenger aboard Sir Thomas Gates' vessel *Sea Venture*. His intent was to set up a business in the new Jamestown colony in Virginia. He planned to bring his wife and family over once he had established himself there. After an almost fatal shipwreck off Bermuda, Hopkins eventually did get to Jamestown only to find a colony in serious disarray. It was clear to Hopkins that he could never prosper in such an atmosphere. He took the first opportunity to leave, sailing home on the ship *Patience*. His later council to John Carver and William Bradford, based on what he had experienced in Jamestown, would prove invaluable to the two leaders as they worked to avoid the same settlement pitfalls in Plimoth.

The Hopkins somehow survived that terrible first winter at Plimoth and the family continued to grow. Years later, William Bradford recorded in his personal journal that Hopkins and his wife "lived about 20 years in this place, and had one son and four daughters borne here ... his son Giles is married and hath four children ... his daughter Constanta (Constance) is also married, and hath 12 children, all of them living."

In 1638, Stephen Hopkins was granted permission to relocate himself to Yarmouth, albeit briefly. The Plimoth court, on August 7 of that year, allowed him to "erect a house at Mattacheese, and cut hay to winter his cattle, provided it be not to withdraw from the Town of Plimoth." His small house was located in the western section of what is now Yarmouth Port. At the time, he was the only white settler in the area. The record indicates that he was back in Plimoth after his short stay on the Cape. Clearly still an entrepreneur, he was fined in September for selling beer, wine, and "strong waters" at what was deemed an excessive price.

Hopkins' son Giles, who was about ten years of age when he crossed the Atlantic with his family, arrived at Yarmouth in 1639 as one of the town's earliest permanent settlers. By the end of the year he was married to Catherine Wheldon, the daughter of Gabriel Wheldon of neighboring Barnstable. Giles and his bride may have started their married life in the elder Hopkins' house. Yet, within five years the Hopkins family relocated to Barnstable, and still later they moved again to Nauset (along what is now Tonset Road in Orleans near Town Cove.) Giles's sister Constance had earlier settled at Nauset in 1644 with her husband Nicholas Snow. That same year, Stephen, the patriarch, died at Plimoth.

As for Giles, he lived to the ripe age of 80, dying in 1690 as one of the last surviving *Mayflower* Pilgrims. Both he and his sister are buried in the Old Cove Cemetery in Eastham.

Squanto's Sad End
Anyone familiar with the Pilgrim story knows how the Indian Squanto helped them to survive in their new environment. The fortuitous arrival in Plimoth of this English-speaking Native American in the spring of 1621 seemed to the Pilgrims as almost like a gift of Divine Providence. Speaking for them all, William Bradford recorded that Squanto "was a special instrument sent of God for their good beyond their expectation."

But Squanto's place in Pilgrim history is actually rather clouded and his eventual fall from grace is not a topic which gets much coverage in the history books. In fact, his star rose and fell quickly. Just a year later when he died, the person who had acted as the helpful intermediary between the Pilgrims and the Wampanoags was accorded neither a resting place within the English community that he had adopted, nor among the sacred burial places of his own people.

Squanto, or Tisquantum as he was known by his Indian compatriots, had been captured on Cape Cod by English Captain Thomas Hunt in 1614. He was taken to Spain and from what we know, was sold there as a servant. Somehow he ended up in England and was eventually taken by fishermen to the coast of Maine. From there, he walked back to the region that his tribe had inhabited near Plimoth. When he got there, he found that in his absence a pestilence had killed all of the members of his tribe. He took refuge with Massasoit, then sachem of the Wampanoags. When Massasoit learned of the arrival of the Pilgrims, he directed Squanto to present himself and assist these Englishmen.

Massasoit had reasons for doing this. Facing a large and vigorous tribe of Narragansetts to his west, Massasoit desired the military power of the English to protect his tribe from the incursions of his more aggressive neighbors. He knew that if he could convince the Pilgrims that there was a mutual interest in keeping the Narragansetts on the defensive, then his own tribe would benefit. Thus the reason why Squanto was sent to cement relations with the Pilgrims. Largely through Squanto's efforts, the Wampanoags were able to enlist the Pilgrims as an ally and a peace treaty was signed by both parties pledging to aid each other in the case of trouble.

It didn't take long, however, before Squanto apparently tried to make himself far more important in the grand scheme of things than either the Pilgrims or Massasoit had envisioned. Believing that the debt the Pilgrims owed him for their survival during that first year made him essential to them, he began to exact small payments of various sort from them. And he did the same to the Indians. As William Bradford later put it, "... Squanto sought his own ends, and played his own game, by putting the Indians in fear and drawing gifts from them to enrich himself; making them believe that he could stir up war against whom he would, and make peace for whom he would."

Squanto claimed to have the power to release a plague on the Indians, telling them he learned the secret from the Pilgrims. And he also told the Indians that he could control whether the Pilgrims would stay faithful as allies in the event of a war. Squanto's initial popularity and continued influence with the Pilgrims raised a powerful envy in Massasoit and the sachem made no secret that he would not be upset if Squanto suddenly disappeared from the scene. After Squanto allegedly initiated a false claim that Massasoit was planning to attack the Pilgrims, the Wampanoag leader demanded that the settlers turn him over for execution. They refused.

Realizing that he had overplayed his hand, Squanto stayed very close to the Pilgrims for protection. He claimed to have adopted Christianity and continued to act as a guide and interpreter as the English explored the areas around Plimoth and Cape Cod. In the fall of 1622, while guiding the Pilgrims near Chatham, Squanto became ill and died. Bradford described the death of his Indian friend. "In this place Squanto fell sick of an Indian fever, bleeding much at the nose, and within a few days, died there desiring that we pray for him that he might go to the Englishman's God in heaven." Pray for him they no doubt did, but the body of Squanto was not buried in Plimoth, nor was it given a place of honor among his own people. Instead, his remains lie in an unmarked and uncelebrated grave somewhere at the Cape's foggy elbow.

Plymouth Rock: America's First National Monument

Displayed in a cage along the water's edge at Plymouth Harbor is perhaps the most famous rock in the United States. True, there are other important boulders around the country, like Chimney Rock in Wyoming and Courthouse Rock in Idaho—and certainly bigger ones like Stone Mountain in Georgia. But Plymouth Rock has a special place in America's consciousness above all others because it was from here, the story goes, that a nation was born.

On a bleak and cold December day in 1620, the Pilgrims made a landfall at Plymouth Harbor. Subsequent attempts to capture that moment have given way to elaborate scenes of thankful Pilgrims standing in prayer on a rock as they survey the forbidding landscape before them. As a symbol of endurance, the monolith has sanctified the Pilgrim experience. It has become a metaphor to reinforce and extol the values of New England Protestantism. And for over three hundred and fifty years it has served as a sort of symbolic cornerstone of our nation.

Why this particular chunk of granite achieved such fame stems from a claim by Elder Thomas Faunce. Faunce was the son of John Faunce, who had come to Plymouth in 1623 aboard the ship *Anne*. In 1741, when the town was planning to put a wharf near the original landing site, Thomas Faunce told the town fathers that, as a child, some of the original Pilgrims had pointed out the rock to him as the place where they had taken their first step in the New World. "Here was the very spot," he said, "which had received the footsteps of our fathers on their first arrival." Apparently, everyone seemed to have forgotten the fact that the first Pilgrim steps had been taken at Provincetown. But, based on the then 94-year-old churchman's second hand testimony, the rock was saved.

During the Revolutionary War, patriot groups in Plymouth attempted to move the rock closer to the town center as a base for a liberty pole. Unfortunately, in the moving process, the boulder

split in half. Some interpreted this as a symbol of the split between
the colonies and Great Britain. On the 200th anniversary of the
Pilgrim landing, in 1820, Daniel Webster delivered a speech in front
of the rock that forever enshrined it and the values of the
Forefathers in American mythology. Webster cited "their sufferings,
our gratitude for their labors, our admiration for their virtues, our
veneration of their piety, and our attachment to those principles of
civil and religious liberty for which they encountered the dangers
of the ocean, the storms of heaven, the violence of the savages, disease, exile, and famine to enjoy and to establish ... " this nation.
Fourteen years later, this remnant of the rock was relocated to the
front yard of Pilgrim Hall and placed inside an iron fence. In 1880,
the piece that had broken off and which was serving as a doorstop
for a warehouse was reunited with its more celebrated half and
cemented back together. The rock was moved to the waterfront and
given a stone canopy and some Greek pillars to set it off.

By the time of the 300th anniversary of the Pilgrim landing, in
1920, Plymouth Rock had come under the jurisdiction of the
National Society of Colonial Dames. Under their auspices, the rock
was moved again to its present waterfront site—once more with
bits and pieces breaking off it—and enclosed in an elaborate
Grecian temple.

Plymouth Rock. (Jim Coogan collection)

Still, even with all this veneration, not everyone has treated the rock with reverence or respect. George Willison, who wrote the classic book *Saints and Strangers*, claims that the Plymouth town fathers concocted the story about the landing as a marketing campaign to bring the tourists to town. For Willison, the rock sits in its shorefront enclosure, " ... dreaming perhaps of other days when it was not gathering moss and peanuts, and odd bits of lunch tossed at it by casual sightseers ... "

Others actually expressed their feelings about Plymouth Rock with acts of vandalism. In 1937, someone painted the rock red. No one was apprehended. But when the same thing happened a year later, the Plymouth police department eventually arrested a workman who painted water towers around the south shore. The culprit claimed that he had no political agenda and had only done the deed "just for fun." Nevertheless, he was fined and spent some time in jail for his desecration of the symbol. In the 1950's, Provincetown poet Harry Kemp "bombed" the rock with sacks of flour to protest Plymouth's unwillingness to acknowledge that the Cape tip was where the Pilgrims first landed.

Over time, Plymouth Rock has meant a number of things to different groups. It has been used as a symbol for a breed of chickens and even as the brand for a type of working man's pants. Cynics have questioned its authenticity as a genuine historic relic, and many tourists have been less than impressed by its small size. But, its continued veneration might perhaps be best measured by the many sales of "authentic" pieces that now occur on eBay. After all these years, Plymouth Rock is still the biggest attraction in "America's home town." And thousands make the trek each year to see it.

Provincetown's Pilgrim Monument

On August 5, 1908, when Mrs. Rosilla Bangs left her home to pick up some groceries on Commercial Street, she had no idea that she would become a footnote in the building of the Provincetown Monument. On that morning as Mrs. Bangs made her way across the street, a railcar, used for hauling granite for the building, broke loose and rolled down the hill from the construction site, crushing her to death. Interestingly, she became the only casualty in the three-year building program that created the tallest all-granite structure in the United States. This small footnote is just one of many fascinating facts that attach to one of the Cape's most memorable landmarks.

The late nineteenth century spawned a number of monument building programs around the nation. The period brought a number of commemorations for various themes in American history. Descendants of the Pilgrims had always wanted some kind of physical memento of the 1620 voyage to North America. Cape Codders, in particular, wanted to make sure that the fact that the Pilgrims made their initial landfall at Provincetown would not be lost. In 1852, a group was formed to put some kind of memorial at the Cape tip but it was unable to secure support from the Massachusetts legislature for such an endeavor. The best that could be done was to put a small plaque on High Pole Hill next to the Provincetown town hall.

A more serious effort was mounted in 1877 with a call from the Cape Cod Association for the active solicitation of state and federal funding for a significant commemorative to the Pilgrims at Provincetown. A 70-foot stone building was proposed which would feature a lighted clock and a storm signal. However, despite periodic attempts to push for public funding, the group's efforts amounted to little more than annual meetings. In 1892, the Cape Cod Pilgrim Memorial Association was formed but it wasn't until almost ten years later, when Captain Joseph Henry Sears of Brewster grabbed the reins of the organization, that things began to progress. Sears, a prominent shipmaster and owner of several vessels, was a dynamic personality. As president of the association, he began an intense and eventually successful campaign to raise funds for a major construction. From 1901, when Sears became involved, until 1907 when actual construction began, the treasury of the association grew from $1,200 to over $100,000. Sears concentrated his efforts in Washington, D C., eventually persuading Congress to pledge $40,000 for the memorial. The remainder of the funding was done privately. Prominent Americans donated to the cause. Among them was Andrew Carnegie who wrote a check for $1,000.

Without any firm plans as to what the actual monument would look like, but confident that it was time to begin, preparations for leveling the site and constructing a stone base for a building began in the spring of 1907. The actual location of the monument was never an issue. High Pole Hill had become available after a fire destroyed the Provincetown town hall in the late 1870's and townspeople had decided not to rebuild on that exposed spot. At 100 feet above sea level, the hill was the perfect spot as it dominated the town and the harbor in front of it. As the committee deliberated on various designs, there were many ideas, some practical, and some far out of the realm of possibility. Captain Sears himself seemed to have no set idea as to what kind of a design should prevail. When asked, he indicated that the building would be "nothing elaborate" but made of stone and "just as high as possible." A study commission was formed that settled on, of all things, a replica of the municipal building of Sienna Italy, the Torre del Mangia. Even when the cornerstone for the monument was laid on June 20, 1907, with President Theodore Roosevelt doing the honors, it appears that few—even those on the committee—realized just how imposing the building would actually be.

A contract was let to the firm of Maguire and O'Heron of Milton, Massachusetts. For $73,865 (exclusive of the foundation which was already in place) the company agreed to complete the work by December of 1909. There was a five-dollar-a-day penalty for work not complete beyond this date. In the spring of 1908 construction began in earnest.

As the building went up, over 100 memorial stones from around the nation were incorporated within the walls. One stone came from the church at Austerfield, England where William Bradford had been baptized and where the original Pilgrim movement began. Another came from the church at Leyden in Holland. There was no outside scaffolding. Timbers were placed inside of the tower as it rose to support a steam-powered crane. Stones were brought from the pier up the hill by a temporary railway. It was one of those cars that caused the death of Mrs. Bangs. At ground level, the walls of the monument are five feet thick, tapering to three feet in the upper portion. Each corner is anchored with heavy cables connected to the eight-foot thick reinforced concrete base.

During the winter of 1908-1909 construction was suspended for the weather. The following spring, the outside of the memorial was completed with the last exterior stone put in place on August 21, 1909. The interior of the building, including the 60 incline ramps, was finished from the top down. Workers re-used the interim wooden framework for support as they moved down the inside of the tower. The building was ready for dedication on August 5, 1910. The date reflected when the Pilgrims has sailed from Southampton, England in 1620. President William Howard Taft presided over a gala celebration, which included the illumination of the 252-foot structure with over 1,000 lights. The attending US naval fleet and all of the major buildings in Provincetown were similarly illuminated. For those who attended the ceremony, it was an unforgettable experience.

And this is true of people who climb the structure today.

Chapter 2

Slices of Cape Life

Forging a life in days of old was no small task. Slices of local life can be seen in the foods the people ate, the beasts and diseases they faced, and even the village taverns where they relaxed with a pint and some friendly conversation.

Cape Cod Grown

Henry David Thoreau visited Cape Cod during the mid-19th century, noting that the landscape in many places was largely devoid of trees due to the wood needed to build ships, to build and heat homes, and to feed the salt making industry (earlier using wood to build fires to boil away saltwater; later to build salt vats across the Cape). As a result, the lack of trees allowed the winds to strip away the fertile topsoil. This was not good news for area farmers.

Even before the trees were felled, the soil of Cape farms never possessed the degree of richness as at more inland farms. Along the north side of the peninsula, where the soil was less sandy than in the south, corn yield was about 30 bushels per acre (20 bushels per acre along the more sandy south). Compare these figures to farms in the heartland where some 100 bushels were harvested per acre. Yet, interestingly, at the turn of the 20th century, "farmer" was listed as the most popular occupation in the town of Orleans—in fact, twice as popular as the occupation "fisherman."

Corn and other grains such as rye were popular as evidenced by the large number of windmills located throughout the peninsula during the 19th century. Salt hay was harvested from the marshes for use as fodder for livestock. Along the lower Cape, in Eastham, farmers grew asparagus and turnips. In fact, during the first half of the 20th century these farmers became the state's largest producers of asparagus. Turnips were well known to European settlers as a popular crop of their native continent. The Cape's light soil and cool climate made for an ideal environment in which to cultivate the vegetable.

The conditions on Cape Cod were especially ideal for cranberry cultivation—with its unique combination of swampy bogs and sandy soil. Cranberries were a valuable food source for the Natives and the early settlers, as the tangy berries which grew wild in the wetlands provided valuable Vitamin C. Locals, including Henry Hall of Dennis, discovered that sand mixed with bog soil helped to aerate the peat and enhanced the berries' growth. From that discovery and further experiments grew the cranberry industry.

And to keep the doctor away, apple orchards were part of the Cape landscape as noted by Thoreau during one of his four visits to the area.

Attack of the Wolves

Cape Cod of old was a dark wilderness where terrible beasts lurked behind trees and bushes, ready to pounce. Amongst these were wolves that feasted on the settlers' livestock. William Wood, in his 1634 book *New England's Prospect*, provided a snapshot of the New World, writing in a section entitled "Of the Beasts that Live on the Land" that, "The wolves be in some respect different from them in other countries. It was never known yet that a wolf ever set upon a man or woman. Neither do they trouble horses or cows; but swine, goats, and red calves, which they take for deer, be often destroyed by them."

Wood's description of the wolves of the area reads as follows: "They be made much like a mongrel, being big boned, lank paunched, deep breasted, having a thick neck and head, prick ears, and long snout, with dangerous teeth, long-staring hair, and a great bush tail ... Sometimes ten or twelve are of a company. Late at night and early in the morning they set up their howlings and call their companies together—at night to hunt, at morning to sleep."

Wood referred to wolves as "the greatest inconveniency the country hath, both for matter of damage to private men in particular, and the whole country in general." Pilgrim William Bradford agreed with Wood, as he wrote in 1624 in his journal *Of Plimoth Plantation*, "The country is annoyed with foxes and wolves ... but poison, traps and other such means will help to destroy them." Wolves were indeed a menace. Historian Frederick Freeman, in his *History of Cape Cod—Volume I & II* (published in 1860 and 1862), makes numerous mention of the local colonists' battles with the wolves of the area. Referring to the 17th century he wrote, "Wolves making great depredations upon herds and flocks, wolf-traps were ordered by the colony court to be made." Bounties were offered for the killing of troublesome wolves. For instance, in 1655 four wolves were killed in Sandwich, six in Yarmouth, nine in Barnstable, and four in Eastham. The year 1685 saw "the towns continuing to be infested by (wolves) to the great annoyance of the inhabitants and doing much damage by destruction of sheep and cattle."

In the 18th century, local towns continued to wrestle with the wolf problem. A $50 bounty (a huge sum in those early days) was offered in Barnstable, while Falmouth, Sandwich, Wareham, and Plymouth teamed up to offer a $60 reward for the head of one troublesome wolf. Sandwich mustered "every able-bodied man" to hunt wolves and the problem became so widespread that it was proposed to construct a fence from Cape Cod Bay to Buzzards Bay in order to prevent wolves from entering Sandwich. Off-Cape towns filed their opposition with the General Court and the fence was not built.

The names of some Cape landmarks point to the wolf problem, such as Wolf Hill Pond in Harwich and Wolf Trap Neck in Sandwich, while local farmers transported their livestock either to fenced necks or offshore islands, such as Hog Island, for grazing.

Wolves still caused problems during the 19th century. In 1827, the town of Sandwich offered a $100 bounty according to Freeman for "the killing of a wolf that was causing destruction of sheep." Author Edward Rowe Snow, in his book *A Pilgrim Returns to Cape Cod*, mentions a wolf that was suspected of killing 3,000 sheep during its lifetime! That wolf was eventually shot by a Sandwich farmer.

Though today wolves are no longer part of the Cape's wildlife scene, there has been a dramatic increase in the number of coyotes across the peninsula. Perhaps it is time to build that fence!

The Smallpox Fine

Centuries ago, Cape residents and those throughout Massachusetts and New England lived in fear of smallpox—a deadly disease felt throughout colonial times and into the early years of the 19th century. Diseases such as smallpox, brought by early explorers that visited these shores and by European fishermen that worked the local waters, had earlier decimated the Native Indians of the area even before the Pilgrims arrived on the scene. In the decades following the *Mayflower's* arrival Cape communities battled with the disease, in many cases being able to contain the pox to a handful of families until the scare was eventually thwarted. Other communities, though, found themselves faced with a growing epidemic. One of the worst smallpox outbreaks on Cape took place in Chatham during 1765/66 when nearly 40 members of the community died. Among them was the town's physician, Dr. Samuel Lord.

Communities went to great lengths to contain the disease. Inflicted members were segregated from the population. After death, the victim's clothing and bedclothes were burned. And the bodies of the deceased were quickly buried in separate burial grounds.

Nineteenth century historian Frederick Freeman, in his book *History of Cape Cod*, states that, "In 1778, the small-pox in (Sandwich) caused much alarm. A 'pest-house' was provided, the roads near and around it were 'fenced-up,' nurses who had had the disease were provided, a 'red flag hung at the fencings,' all intrusion upon the grounds was prohibited, and even the cats and dogs running at large were killed to prevent contagion."

When the disease arrived in Eastham during the 1760's officials there levied a fine against anyone who came into contact with the disease and kept the knowledge of that exposure a secret. According to Freeman: "Exposure to the ravages of small-pox, at this time, induced an application ... to authorize a fine of any persons who, having been exposed to the infection, and having knowledge of the fact, should neglect to give timely notice to the selectmen."

Today, along the Cape's byways, many times hidden from view, rest the lonely smallpox cemeteries. The common dates on the stones point to the scourge that visited the communities

Grave of Dr. Samuel Lord, smallpox victim. (Jack Sheedy photo)

and the similar surnames hint of the sadness that hung over many families.

The Colonial Meeting House
In the early days of settling Cape Cod, when a community was being established, the first structure that was put up was the meeting house. The building served as a place of worship and also as a town hall where governing decisions were made by the male freemen. For most of the late seventeenth and early eighteenth centuries the two functions were intertwined.

The meeting house belonged to the town and in its function as a church there were specific guidelines as to how people were to be seated. Initially, the pews were allocated by a committee that met yearly. To take a non-assigned seat could bring a penalty. By the latter part of the 1700's pews were commonly sold to members of the congregation. The first bid for a spot was reserved for the man who had paid the highest annual land tax the previous year. The choicest "seats for distinction" were always located closest to the minister's pulpit. These went for the highest price. Almost like a modern day sports draft, a man could make an arrangement with a neighbor to trade up or down for a select position. In addition to the family pews, there was a special place for the minister's wife. There was also a section set aside for elderly men and women who may have lacked any family connections. Children did not generally sit with their parents in church, but on low side seats in the aisles, as near them as convenience would admit. If there was a gallery, it was reserved for servants and Indians.

The 1796 construction of the new meeting house in the north parish of Harwich is illustrative of how the seating inside the meeting house corresponded to the price of where the prime locations were. For the honor of sitting closest to the pulpit, Captain Kimbal Clark paid $224 for a pew on the west side of the building. Captain Elijah Cobb paid $204 for the pew just to the east side of the pulpit. On pews located further away from the front of the building, the price dropped correspondingly. These pieces of religious real estate were treated just like any other piece of property in that they were annually taxed and became part of the estate of the owner. The pew deeds to the church in Centerville, for example, covered four pages in the town record book. Pews were left in wills to the designated heirs, "as long as the Meeting House lasts."

Occasionally, the sale of pews caused problems. Families without much money would pool their funds to share the cost of a seat. In 1784, Kenelm Winslow and Nathan Winslow paid six pounds, six shillings for "two thirds of one third of a pew" in the North Parish meeting house in Harwich. Over time, these mixed titles became the source of family feuds as descendants tried to sort out the seating order. John Cole of Eastham brought a suit in 1776 claiming that his pew had been cut nine inches too short and that it unfairly gave extra space to the Kenrick family.

Many of the pew owners were sea captains. When they were away—which was often, most of them generously allowed others to use their pews. After all, they didn't need them. But on one occasion this arrangement ran into problems. Captain Edward Penniman, a prominent whaler from Eastham, owned an expensive pew in the Methodist Church. When he returned one time from a long whaling voyage he found that the church elders had rented out his pew to another family rather than just giving them free use of it. Angry at the actions of those he had trusted in his absence, Captain Penniman decided that the fiscal practicality of his Methodist brethren was not in the spirit of what he saw as proper Christian charity. He gave up his pew and left the church to become a Universalist.

Taverns, Taprooms, and Temperance

Since the earliest colonial times, taverns and public pouring houses have been part of the social fabric of Cape Cod. The Pilgrims actually drank more beer than water while on board the *Mayflower* and early communities tolerated alcohol consumption as long as it did not interfere with the hard work of colony building.

One of the first local tavern keepers was Thomas Huckins of Barnstable who was regularly filling glasses in the mid-1600's with rum brought from Boston on his packet ship. As the proprietor of a tavern, Huckins was considered no less an upright citizen than anyone else in town and the record shows that he was elected to the post of selectman seven times by his fellow citizens. In 1715, when the Reverend Hugh Adams of Chatham raised questions about the

appropriateness of pouring houses in the town, he found himself at
odds with Ebenezer Hawes. Hawes was a popular citizen and he
represented the majority feelings in Chatham. He was also the
town's first tavern keeper. Through Hawes' influence, Adams was
given his walking papers. Residents declared the ministry to be
vacant and called for his replacement.

Cape Codders quaffed large quantities of spirits in those early
days. Liquor was both plentiful and inexpensive and there were
numerous social occasions to bring out the jug. Weddings, community gatherings, ship launchings, christenings, even the ordination
of a new minister, were excuses for the use of "ardent spirits."
Sickness brought prescriptions of alcohol-based remedies that, if
they did nothing else, made being ill a bit less uncomfortable.
Operations were never done without whiskey being present.

Along the route to the Lower Cape there were a number of
popular watering holes for travelers. A 1644 Massachusetts law
actually required towns to keep a public house. In Sandwich, there
was Fessenden's and Newcomb's. Further west, in Barnstable
Village there were actually three taverns. Cornelius Crocker, Jr. ran
an establishment at Sunset Lane. His father, Cornelius Crocker, Sr.

Shattuck House, Orleans. (Jim Coogan collection)

had another opposite the old Sturgis homestead, and Otis Loring had still another one right at the foot of Rendezvous Lane. The Yarmouth Tavern near Summer Street in Yarmouth Port was a popular stopping point and people that left the north side to go over to Harwich could find lodging, food, and drink at the Atlantic House. In Brewster, Thomas Winslow, David Bangs, and Nathaniel Howes were licensed in 1758 "to keep a public house for entertainment." Around this time, Nathaniel Stone and Theophilis Hopkins, also of Brewster, were given permission to sell "strong drink" out of their houses. In Orleans, Simeon Higgins ran a public house where one delighted visitor was astonished to report that the sleeping rooms were furnished with "the best of hair mattresses throughout." Holbrook's Hotel in Wellfleet provided a break before reaching Provincetown where there were more than a half a dozen establishments that could slack the thirst of a weary traveler.

But too much of a good thing eventually brought a reaction. Whereas the 18th century had seemed far more tolerant to tippling, the 1800's produced a time of reform among Cape Codders. There was increasing opposition to the presence of taverns and pouring houses by groups of citizens who believed that alcohol brought as much sadness to the community as it did pleasure.

Perhaps it was indeed time to take some action. By the early nineteenth century, Yarmouth boasted seventeen places where alcohol could be obtained on the north side of town alone. And these establishments were serving a population that numbered not much more than 2,000 people! Working with the forces of temperance was the great religious revival spirit of the period. In March of 1817, a number of Yarmouth citizens convened "for the purpose of taking into consideration the excessive and ruinous use of spirituous liquors, which has become so generally prevalent among all classes of people, and for adopting some measures to prevent or check the pernicious practice." The Yarmouth Association for the Suppression of Intemperance was the second such organization in Massachusetts. Almost 100 men of "good character" signed the original charter and pledged to fight "poverty, wretchedness and gross immorality which at the present day so greatly abounds among us." Dennis and Sandwich had groups that followed a similar path of opposition to alcohol consumption.

Up through the 1850's a number of temperance societies were created on Cape Cod. The rising tide of Methodism and its strong stand against liquor, coupled with a distaste of the hard drinking habits of the newer immigrant groups, drove the movement. Towns began to seize private stores of liquor, provoking many protests and court cases that challenged these intrusions. It became more difficult to locate some "flip" and "toddy." The Civil War itself provided some relief for those who sought alcohol as it was often the only diversion for soldiers when they were away from the horrors of that conflict and there was less condemnation of drinking.

With the war's end, the national temperance organization known as the Good Templars began to spread across Cape Cod. The Henry Wilson Lodge of Good Templars was formed in South Dennis in 1867 by a group who called themselves "friends of good order and morals." A similar group met in St. Elmo's Hall in Dennisport. In Harwichport, the Satucket Lodge of Good Templars was organized in 1888. South Yarmouth had its own branch in the Victory Lodge of Good Templars, formed in 1887.

Hyannis had two organizations, the Dawn of Truth Good Templars and the Sons of Temperance. In Provincetown, the Sons of Temperance: Mayflower Division and its sister group, the Daughters of the Ocean Wave Temperance Union worked hard to cleanse the Cape tip of alcohol.

Clearly, these nineteenth century temperance groups formed the basis for the passage of the national prohibition movement that came later in the twentieth century. The 18th amendment attempted to eliminate forever the influence of alcohol in the United States. By the time of its passing, most Cape towns had already voted themselves "dry" and many stayed that way even after the sale of alcohol was again legalized in the 1930's. And although bootlegging and clandestine roadhouses were admittedly part of the 1920's Cape social scene, it wasn't until the new post-World War II tourist boom that the respectability of pouring houses was re-established. In hindsight, we can look at the idealistic efforts of the temperance groups as being probably preordained to failure. The history of America shows that for every Billy Sunday, there are at least ten people like Ebenezer Hawes.

Severe Weather on Cape Cod

The Cape has seen its share of wild weather over the centuries, adding ever-darkening hues to the canvas of this area's long historical mural. Hundreds of storms, blizzards and nor'easters have come from out of the Atlantic to wreak havoc, some of them causing destruction and loss of life.

In fact, just fifteen years after the Pilgrims' arrival, and just a few years before the Cape's settlement, the area was visited by a severe hurricane. It arrived in August of 1635, inflicting much damage to the coastal regions. Governor William Bradford wrote in his journal of the event: "such a mighty storme of wind and raine as none living in these parts, either English or Indeans ever saw... and made many of the Indeans to clime into trees for their saftie." This storm severely damaged the Pilgrims' trading post on Buzzards Bay. It's believed that perhaps two more major hurricanes arrived in the northeast during the 17th century, and at least four during the 18th century.

Hurricanes were not the only destructive forces to reach these shores. The great October Gale of 1841 sank many local ships, killing 57 mariners from Truro alone, and more than 20 from Dennis. In 1862, a February gale ripped the roof off the Agricultural Hall at the Barnstable Fairgrounds. In 1867, a January storm toppled barns and crumbled brick chimneys. In 1870, a waterspout tormented mariners at Barnstable Harbor, sinking at least one boat before eventually making landfall to cause damage at Josiah Hinckley's lumberyard. And in 1871, a lightning bolt struck the Universalist Church on Main Street, Hyannis, setting it afire and eventually bringing about its destruction. Not to be outdone, an October 1878 storm was strong enough to topple the steeples of two Barnstable churches in town, to the dismay of Unitarians and Baptists alike.

Winters of the past were especially harsh on our ancestors. During one particular winter near the end of the 17th century there were more than 30 storms. While the winter of 1780 was so cold that Barnstable Harbor froze over thick enough for Nathaniel Gorham to lead his four oxen across with a load of firewood from Sandy Neck to the mainland. Yet, the wildest weather arrived during 1816 following a severe winter. Frost occurred during each

month of the year, with ice as late as May. Many places throughout
New England recorded a fall of snow in June. On Cape Cod,
Barnstable's corn crop was destroyed in September by a frost.
Other crops were harvested earlier than usual, resulting in lesser
yields and higher prices.

The winter of 1875 was another cold one, with more than a foot
of ice reported at Cape area harbors. While the winter of 1881 again
froze local harbors sufficiently enough to allow residents to walk
across Barnstable Harbor to Sandy Neck.

Bass River Ferry

The graceful arch of the Bass River Bridge connects the villages of
South Yarmouth and West Dennis. From this point the river twists
inland into the midsection of Cape Cod. Along these shores, centuries ago, Natives dug shellfish evidenced by unearthed shell
heaps. During the Revolutionary War, local vessels were hidden
from the British at coves along the river. Today, fishermen and
boaters enjoy the inland waterway that leads out into the waters of
Nantucket Sound.

But for those folks centuries ago, simply attempting to make
their way either east or west from Point A to Point B, the river was
a huge hurdle to be crossed. The first bridge was not built here until
well into the 19th century. Until that time, travelers required the
services of David Kelly and his river ferry.

Kelly employed members of his family on both sides of the
river to work the ferry. Passage was two cents; two bits for a horse
and carriage. Author/historian Nancy Thacher Reid, in her book
Dennis, Cape Cod: From Firstcomers to Newcomers, 1639-1993, writes:
"The vessel used was a barge, which was poled across, requiring
strong muscles and good balance. The brothers Kelley lived near
the river on the Dennis side and could be summoned to carry passengers by blowing a horn fashioned from a large conch shell, it is
said."

Of course, the building of the first bridge in the 1830's—a toll
bridge—put the ferry out of business. Later, the towns of
Yarmouth, Dennis, and Harwich purchased the wooden bridge,
thus removing the toll and making it a free conveyance. The current bridge was constructed during the years of the Great

Depression as part of the Federal Emergency Administration of Public Works.

On busy summer days, with bumper-to-bumper traffic trying to make it over the Bass River Bridge, just be thankful the ferry is not still in operation. On second thought, any little bit might help!

Village Almshouse

Before welfare and social security, it was the town's responsibility to provide shelter and food for the less fortunate members of the community. Across the Cape, as in other communities throughout New England, the poor, ill, and elderly members of society were placed into the homes of families in town who were paid to look after them. This plan was not always successful, for some were more in it for the money than to provide needed services.

Later, "poor houses," or almshouses, were built to provide a physical location to place those who had nowhere else to go. The *1880 Atlas of Barnstable County* reveals a "Town Farm" in Sandwich located in the vicinity of Charles Street, midway between Sandwich Village and Spring Hill. The "Town Farm," as it was called, was the location of the town's almshouse.

Yarmouth Almshouse. (Courtesy Historical Society of Yarmouth)

Built prior to the American Revolution, the original structure was somewhat tiny, yet was enlarged over the decades with additions until it could sleep more than 20 people. The "Tramp House," added after the Civil War, housed vagrants. Overall, living conditions were simple, but it provided a home to those who could not manage otherwise and provided meals to ward off hunger. Though there were no indoor bathrooms, there was an outhouse provided. Bedding was not entirely vermin-free. Bathing was uncommon, especially among the men. A farm on the grounds tended by residents provided food for their meals. And when their lives were over the residents were buried in unmarked graves at a cemetery also located on the grounds.

Though townsfolk tended to avoid the area, they were good about providing the necessary funding to keep it in operation and to pay the salary of the almshouse keeper. The almshouse eventually closed its doors just after the turn of the 20th century and was later destroyed by fire.

Dennis' almshouse was situated along what is now Old Bass River Road, and was in use from the mid-1800s into the 20th century. It is remembered by the aptly named Almshouse Road. In the neighboring town, an almshouse was located in the village of Yarmouth Port off Center Street, just beyond the ancient cemetery (in the vicinity of another "Almshouse Road"). Its location is shown on the *1880 Atlas of Barnstable County*, identified as "Town Alms H." Built in the 1830's, the facility's budget provided for not only housing and food, but also heating costs, medical attention, and burial expenses. Under keeper Stephen Sherman's guidance, the Yarmouth almshouse was clean and the residents were treated with respect. As the number of its residents decreased, the facility was eventually closed in the early part of the 20th century. Like the Sandwich almshouse, the Yarmouth building also burned.

The Tradition of Town Crier
The office of Town Crier has its roots in medieval Europe. The job of the Town Crier was to assemble the mostly illiterate inhabitants and read proclamations from the government or the church. In colonial New England, the custom was not as common, perhaps because the population was fairly well

The Tradition of Town Crier. (Jim Coogan collection)

schooled in reading at an early age and notices were posted by constables.

Provincetown is most closely connected with town criers. And it is the only Cape town that seems to have had them. From the late 1800's and well into the twentieth century, a series of colorful and occasionally controversial personalities manned the position at the Cape tip. Because there were a number of local papers, the dispensing of general news was not the main priority of the town crier. Instead, they heralded short announcements of special events and town meetings.

One of the earliest Provincetown criers was George Washington Ready. Known to residents as the "Professor," Ready made history, not so much for his work as a crier—something he did for decades, but for startling the world in 1886 with his announcement that he had seen an enormous sea monster off Herring Cove. His description of the 300-foot long serpent made national news. Perhaps just as interesting was the fact that his subsequent work as town crier never seemed to cause any problems with his credibility. He was a legendary character. One time Ready was chosen to make a short appearance in a motion picture that was being filmed in Provincetown. Unfortunately, just as he was to make his entrance onto the set the Boston boat arrived. Caught up in the excitement that always surrounded that event, Ready missed his cue and ruined the shot.

Town criers in the early twentieth century served as a vocal and mobile billboard for announcements, both personal and commercial. As writer Mary Heaton Vorse remembered it, crier Walter Smith walked through the narrow streets ringing his bell and giving out information about upcoming social activities. Criers became an arm of the Board of Trade in the 1930's, greeting and directing the growing influx of tourists. They were paid for advertising a particular business and they also received a small stipend from the town. Occasionally a personal announcement might be part of the crier's package. "Attention, Attention," the crier would shout. "Tony Souza's wife has left his bed and board and he is no longer responsible for any debts that she might incur in his behalf." Sometimes a clarification might be needed for something that might have happened the previous day or week. During World

War II, a Portuguese fisherman got into trouble when he came into the harbor with his flag at half-mast. He was not running the Stars and Stripes, but instead had the Portuguese flag halfway up his masthead. Many townspeople initially felt that the act was unpatriotic in a time of war. The next day the town crier clarified what had happened. "Notice! Manuel Costa wants it known that he is as good an American citizen as anybody, having had his citizenship papers thirty years, and three boys to the front. But he will fly the Portuguese flag or any other flag he wants at half mast when he wants bait, bait having nothing to do with patriotism!"

As tourism began to supplant the fishing industry in Provincetown, later criers like Amos Kubik and Arthur Snader would be down by the harbor front to greet the Boston boat. By now, dressed in a retro Pilgrim costume, complete with tall hat, high white silk stockings, and buckle shoes, the crier would hawk the various restaurants and gift shops, ringing the familiar bell while posing for photographs with the day trippers. Kubik once was sent to New York City in the off-season by the Board of Trade to appear on the Kate Smith radio program. He clanged his bell and reminded people that Provincetown, not Plymouth, was really where the Pilgrims had landed.

In the 1960's, as Provincetown readied for its 350th anniversary, Fred Baldwin was designated for the ceremonial post. Along with his announcements of the various doings at the Cape tip, Baldwin would "officially certify" people as honorary Cape Codders, handing them an inscribed scroll in a brief ceremony. For the 1976 national bicentennial celebration, the town appointed Martin Swanson as town crier but the position lapsed after that event until Napoleon Eugene Poyant picked it up in the early 1980's. Dressed in a red cape, Poyant, a retired local baker, strolled the streets giving the weather report and enlightening tourists with bits of local history. A student of the profession, he entered several international contests for town criers, traveling to Canada to represent Provincetown and Cape Cod. Poyant was the last real crier in Provincetown, serving until 1987.

Occasionally the idea of having another town crier in Provincetown comes up. But the town has chosen not to fill the position, despite the offers of some very willing volunteers. Now, only the memories remain of a time when public information came with a loud voice and the clang of a hand held bell.

Thou Shalt Not Harvest Cranberries on the Sabbath

The cultivation of the native cranberry has been a perennial ritual on Cape Cod for nearly 200 years. Each year the cycle begins anew, with green berries growing beneath the summer sun, ripening to red with the dry days and cool nights of September. The crimson shade tells the locals harvest time is near and by late September and into the month of October workers descend upon the bogs to dry or wet harvest this year's crop.

As with all Cape towns, cranberry picking was serious business in Yarmouth during the 19th century. In those days of old it was not uncommon for whole villages to turn out in order to ensure that the harvest was completed. During the last century, cranberry pickers were hired by growers to perform the physical labor associated with the harvest. Sometimes these pickers were migrant workers (many being Cape Verdean) who made their way from bog to bog throughout southeastern Massachusetts.

Yet, even with the importance of the harvest, for some time cranberry picking was forbidden on Sundays in the town of Yarmouth. Some growers broke the law, and were caught, including

Thou Shalt Not Harvest Cranberries on the Sabbath. (Jim Coogan collection)

the story of one South Yarmouth grower who was brought to court because his pickers were found to be working on the Sabbath. Edwin White, who maintained a crew of several hundred pickers, claimed he was just trying to complete the harvest before the first frost. He was found guilty, and that decision was reaffirmed at the Supreme Court level.

Eventually, a law was passed in the 20th century that made cranberry harvesting in Yarmouth on the Sabbath legal. One could say the blue laws turned to red—cranberry red, that is.

Chapter 3

Whigs, Tories, & Road Tax Collectors

The peninsula of Cape Cod has created many interesting personalities over the centuries, from Patriots to Tories, and from fiery ministers to simple oystermen. The lives of these legendary Cape Codders have left a lasting impression on the pages of local history and lore.

A Scotsman on Cape Cod
Cape Cod's past is dripping with salty tales of mystery and lore, from the dark doings of 18th century witches to the exploits of dashing pirates that visited these sandy shores. And enveloped within the vague realm that exists somewhere between the dusty pages of history and the cloudy veil of folklore is the odd tale of a ghostly Scotsman—replete with a set of bagpipes—whose spirit supposedly still haunts the dunes along Cape Cod Bay.

Elizabeth Reynard, in her classic book, *The Narrow Land*, writes of a Dr. Matthew Fuller who, during the mid-seventeenth century, served as a physician in Barnstable. Cape historian Frederick Freeman noted that "Doct. Matthew Fuller was the first regular practitioner here, succeeded by his son, Dr. John Fuller. They were both eminent." Both writers mention that Fuller the elder, while a worthy physician, was a man who exhibited more than a few eccentricities.

A son of *Mayflower* Pilgrims Edward and Ann Fuller, Matthew Fuller actually did not come to New England until 20 years after his parents had made the Atlantic crossing. He was 30 years old when he landed in Plimoth and he received a 10-acre land grant because of his connection to his by then deceased parents. Fuller lived in Plimoth for about 10 years and then moved to Cape Cod in

1652, settling near Scorton Neck along the boundary of Sandwich and Barnstable. Just prior to King Philip's War, he was made Surgeon General of the colonial troops and he served as a captain during that conflict.

Forced to travel a great deal in his medical practice, Dr. Fuller was served by a devoted assistant named Robert, who was a Scotsman. Robert was never far from the doctor's side, and acted as a personal servant and loyal confidant to Fuller, perhaps as Watson was to Sherlock Holmes.

One of Dr. Fuller's peculiarities was that he always traveled with his personal valuables. Apparently, he trusted no one. These items took the form of gems and jewels, supposedly totaling the equivalent of $200—a good deal of money on Cape Cod in those days. Around 1678, the good doctor died, and when his estate was probated, his valuables were found to be missing. Suspicion immediately fell upon Robert the Scot.

And, although the Scotsman was never charged, the continuing accusations against his character haunted him to his death. In fact, the whispering campaign that circled around the servant probably contributed to the man's sad end. Robert was so affected by what citizens were saying that he stopped eating and died from starvation. He was buried in unhallowed ground between two stones at Scorton Neck. Legend says that Robert the Scot's tormented spirit still haunts this region of the Cape as it continues to search for the doctor's valuables in an effort to prove the poor servant's innocence.

And on certain breezy nights along that stretch of coastline, perhaps it is the shrieking cry of Scottish pipes that one hears mingled with the wayward winds.

Preaching to the "Praying Indians"

The 17th century was a time of clashing cultures, as English settlers occupied lands where Natives once lived. Amidst this environment stepped men of God who made it their mission to preach to the Native Indians of the area. Two men in particular come to mind— Reverend Richard Bourne on the upper Cape and Reverend Samuel Treat along the lower Cape.

Bourne's missionary work began in 1641 at Sandwich where he helped bring Christianity to the Natives of the area. Though he was not yet an ordained minister, he arrived at the "Kingdome of Marshpee" in 1660 to preach to the hundreds of Natives there in their Algonquian tongue. Besides his preaching duties, he was also a representative of the General Court. This experience helped in later years when Bourne fought and won land battles, eventually securing more than 10,000 acres for the Mashpee Natives. The General Court decided "that no part or parcel of these lands might be bought or sold to any white person without the consent of all the said Indians, not even with the consent of the Court." It then became part of Bourne's mission to provide the Mashpee Natives with the ability to manage their own affairs.

Reverend Bourne's eventual ordination took place in 1670 before his Indian congregation. Within this congregation were four Native preachers, including Simon Popmonet who would eventually succeed him after his death in 1685.

Born in Connecticut and earning his degree from Harvard, Reverend Samuel Treat came to Nauset during the 1670's and remained there for the next four and a half decades. Ministering to all those east of old Yarmouth—a sizable area—he earned £70 annual salary and received twenty acres on Town Cove. He also received an annual allotment of firewood and a share of oil from each whale that beached along the shore. The eldest of 21 children, Reverend Treat fathered 14 of his own!

A fiery minister, his mission was to save souls from damnation, which he accomplished through fire and brimstone sermons. His delivery included thunderous words and much Bible thumping. He certainly gave the "Good Book" quite a beating. Besides saving English souls from the pit of hell, his true mission involved converting the Natives along the lower Cape to Christianity through schooling and sermons. To his credit, he learned the Native tongue, participated in their rituals, and attended their ceremonies. Believing in a notion of home rule, he attempted to provide them with the physical and spiritual tools to achieve this. As a result, the Natives grew to admire their white minister and, according to lore, when Reverend Treat died in the midst of a severe snowstorm in 1717, they tunneled through mighty snowdrifts to give him a proper burial.

Edward Bacon: Barnstable's Intractable Tory

That there was Loyalist sentiment on Cape Cod before and during the Revolutionary War is beyond doubt. Some Cape Codders wanted to continue to petition the crown for redress of grievances. Others believed that direct action was needed. As tensions grew in the days prior to the actual struggle, there seemed little room for compromise. Many Loyalists, believing that their fortunes and even their lives were at risk—an attitude not without some justification, eventually left the Cape for Nova Scotia. Others hoped to quietly ride out the conflict without having to take sides. But one prominent individual not only stayed on Cape Cod but he continued to openly undermine the Patriot cause. And this individual had enough support in his home town not only to maintain his status in the community, but also to be elected four successive times as the town's representative to the Massachusetts Legislature—all the while as the conflict was going on.

Squire Edward Bacon was a powerful man in Barnstable. He had served as town clerk, selectman, and as an elected representative to the General Court. He was a deacon in the East Parish church and served for ten years as an associate justice in the Court of Common Pleas. As one historian put it, "Whatever Squire Bacon said was regarded as law by his neighbors." Stubborn and opinionated, Bacon was not one for compromise and his influence extended beyond a hard core of supporters who could be counted on to take his side in town politics.

When the march of the "Body of the People" moved to shut down the operation of the King's Court over the issue of jury selection in September of 1774, Bacon, who was one of the judges, had not opposed the demonstration. Along with James Otis, Sr., and his son Joseph Otis the clerk, Bacon signed a petition that he would resign his commission rather than carry out any "unconstitutional regulations." But many suspected that Bacon's actions were not the true measure of his feelings about independence. Earlier in the year, he had counseled against the town's purchasing weapons to equip its militia and he had also spoken out against participating in any Committees of Correspondence that were forming across Massachusetts. In 1775, he and his supporters temporarily blocked town meeting efforts to send a representative to the Provincial

Congress that was meeting in Cambridge. Bacon portrayed the leaders of the independence movement as radicals and fools, calling them "the vilest of men." After getting wind of one of Bacon's speeches, Samuel Adams wrote to James Otis, warning him of Bacon's treachery. The Otis family, all staunch Patriots, became bitter enemies of Bacon.

Edward Bacon's power was visibly demonstrated in June of 1776, when he and his supporters persuaded town meeting members against taking a positive vote on supporting the Declaration of Independence. With his political ally Nymphas Marston controlling the meeting as moderator, and backed by other influential citizens like Sturgis Gorham, Samuel Crocker, and Samuel Hinckley, Bacon cowed his fellow townsmen into essentially rejecting the proposal, making Barnstable only one of two towns in New England that did not act favorably on the resolution for independence. Such was the intimidation in the assembly by the Loyalist faction, that more than half of the citizens in attendance were too afraid to even vote on the measure.

Bacon continued to represent Barnstable in the General Court as he had done periodically since 1762 and he was elected again in 1778. But anger had been steadily mounting against him and that spring he was denied a seat in the assembly as "a man unfriendly to the Common Cause." He returned to Barnstable where his allies pushed through a petition at a special town meeting demanding that he be allowed to be seated as the town's representative. When it was clear that the petition had no chance of passing, Bacon resigned. For the rest of the year he made his case to the public though letters and speeches and he was re-elected for the 1779 legislative session. This was a confrontation that the Patriot faction did not intend to lose. When Bacon's appeal to be seated reached the House of Representatives, it was matched by a strong petition signed by opponents from Barnstable and some surrounding towns to have him removed. A Resolution of Expulsion carried 95 to 5.

Less than a month after this second expulsion, Barnstable voters once again elected Bacon. Another petition was drawn up chastising those "ambitious, artful and weak or wicked men" who were unjustly attacking his character. It stated that if Bacon would not be allowed to represent the town, Barnstable would consider itself absolved from tax and military quota obligations until it could have the representative that the majority had chosen. But again, he was denied a seat. Apparently thinking that it could wear the legislature down, the town again chose Bacon as its representative in 1780. Loyalty for this Loyalist was apparently more than just skin deep in his home town. But Bacon had few friends outside of it. For a fourth time, the squire was deemed unacceptable by the House of Representatives. Barnstable remained without a representative for the remainder of the war.

Plagued by continued controversies about his character, and affected by a bitter church fight over his suitability as a church deacon, Bacon's health began to deteriorate. He died in 1783, at age 68. On his tombstone in the Cobb's Hill cemetery it says that his was "a life of great abilities [and] very free in conversation." It is the latter aspect of his personality that undoubtedly cost him a place in history. In Simeon Deyo's *History of Barnstable County*, except for where he is included in an obscure list of office holders, Squire Edward Bacon's life does not rate even a single line.

Tar and Feather

During the years preceding the Revolutionary War there was no shortage of opinions in the town of Barnstable. Whigs (Patriots) and Tories plowed their fields and drank their pints within shouting distance of one another. And it was in the midst of this environment, in the year 1776, that tempers boiled out of control, resulting in the tarring and feathering of the widow Abigail Freeman.

Donald Trayser, in his book *Barnstable: Three Centuries of a Cape Cod Town*, described Freeman as "an outspoken shrewish Tory." Known around the village of Barnstable as Widow Nabby, she ran a general store in which she let her opinions fly from behind the counter. She also had no problem voicing her Loyalist sentiments out on the streets of the village, regardless of whether the person standing before her was Whig or Tory.

At the store she continued to sell British tea, which, because of its high tax, was boycotted by the Patriots. Yet, she was not alone in town in terms of her Loyalist views. Others holding her opinion against breaking with the crown included Donald Parker, Jesse Cobb, tavern owner Otis Loring, and Edward Bacon. Yet, Widow Nabby's fierce Tory stance, and perhaps her big mouth, put her at odds with a number of her fellow villagers, quickly making her the target of their aggression.

According to local lore, a gang of young men entered Freeman's house one night, took her from her bed, and hauled her out into the street. There, she was tarred and feathered and then carried around the streets on a rail. The process of "tarring and feathering" consisted of stripping a person, smearing their skin with a sticky pine tar substance, and then rolling them in feathers. It could take days to remove all the feathers and tar. The process was meant to publicly humiliate the victim. It was certainly a low point in Barnstable's struggle for independence.

Isaac Sears: Cape Cod's Other Patriot

When the subject of the American Revolution is discussed, the name of James Otis of West Barnstable is always mentioned. Known as "The Patriot," Otis made fiery speeches in the years leading up to the actual break with England. These earned him the title of "the Patrick Henry of the North." Otis's influence on the struggle was profound. In his attacks against British policies, better known patriots such as John and Samuel Adams found inspiration and direction for their arguments. But there was another Cape-born man who had just as much influence, and who certainly took an active role from the beginning to the end of the rebellion—something that Otis could not do owing to his being affected by a beating at the hands of a Tory group. That man was Isaac Sears.

Sears was born in West Brewster in July of 1730. He was the son of Joshua and Mary (Thacher) Sears. The family moved to Norwich, Connecticut when Isaac was just a boy. By age 22 the young man was master of his own small vessel trading between New York and Canada. In the French and Indian Wars of the 1750's, Sears commanded a series of privateers, the *Decoy*, the *Catherine*, and also the sloop, *Belle Isle*. After the war he moved his base to New York City. There he made himself a recognized leader along the waterfront. In 1765 he began a series of speeches against the Stamp Act and for the rest of the decade he was active in anti-British activities and a founder of the Sons of Liberty in the city.

Recognized as much for his fists as his speechmaking abilities, Sears played to the populace and was elected to the first Provincial Congress. As leader of the Committee of Safety, he was popularly styled as "King Sears." In 1774 he participated in New York's "tea party," an imitation of Boston's act of defiance of British taxes.

Around that time, the *New York Mercury* published a poem about "King" Sears.

> *"At this time there arose, a certain 'King Sears'"*
> *Who made it his duty, to banish our fears.*
> *He was without doubt, a person of merit,*
> *Great knowledge, some wit, and abundance of spirit,*
> *Could talk like a lawyer, and that without fee,*
> *And threaten'd perdition, to all that drank tea."*

In November of 1775, Sears led a raid on a Loyalist newspaper, destroying the printing presses and driving Tories out of New York City. Arrested and held for a time in prison, Sears was freed by a patriotic mob and paraded through the streets like a hero. There is evidence that he was one of the men who helped pull down the 4,000-pound statue of King George in New York on July 9, 1776.

When the war came and New York City was occupied by British troops, Sears returned to Massachusetts. From 1777 through the end of the war in 1783 he made his home in Boston, promoting privateering and traveling frequently to Cape Cod to visit his extended family. One of the privateers that he financed was the *General Arnold*, which was wrecked in Plymouth Harbor during the winter of 1778.

By the war's end Sears was bankrupt. In an effort to revive his fortunes, he formed a partnership with Captain James Magee and attempted to become involved in the China trade. He sailed with Magee for Canton but became ill while en route. He never recovered and died in October of 1786, shortly after the ship arrived in China.

Isaac Sears left a mixed legacy. As some historians have written, "no epithet was too strong to apply to him." Theodore Roosevelt, writing his history of the Revolution in 1906, called Sears "a 'frothy man,' a noisy braggart, demagogue, and mob leader." Others have been kinder, emphasizing his patriotism and devotion to the cause of liberty.

Whichever way he is viewed, there is little doubt that Isaac "King" Sears was an important figure in America's struggle for independence—and a Cape Codder!

Lucy Rich and the *H.M.S. Somerset*

Sometimes the re-examination of history can reveal that long-told and popular stories are indeed just that—stories. It seems that often a good yarn can trump what really happened. And why not? The real facts may be far less interesting! Historians have to be very careful in sifting myth from reality. For years, most popular Cape history books carried the story that during the American Revolution when the British warship *Somerset* was wrecked off the Truro shore in November of 1778, the ship's surgeon was able to avoid being taken prisoner by agreeing to stay and become the town doctor. The legend also claimed that Dr. William Thayer became a permanent and well respected resident and that he eventually married a local girl named Lucy Rich.

Marjorie Hubble Gibson, in a meticulously researched book on the wreck of the *Somerset*, debunked this romantic tale. Using primary sources from the Public Records Office in London that were apparently overlooked by many earlier writers like Simeon Deyo and more contemporary ones like Henry Kittredge, Gibson established that the ship's surgeon was, in fact, a British citizen named Henry Watson. After capture and a long march to Boston with the rest of the British prisoners, Watson was confined aboard a prison ship in Boston Harbor until his health made his transfer to a private home necessary. Eventually he was exchanged for some captured Americans.

Dr. Thayer was a Cape Codder and was already living in Truro at the time of the wreck. He was also already married to Susanna Rich and was the father of three children. There is some truth that Dr. Thayer had a connection to the wreck of the *Somerset*. He was indeed present when the warship foundered. And he was one of a number of men who submitted salvage claims on the wrecked vessel, later getting a small portion of the proceeds of what had been auctioned off. This may be where the confusion originated. But the rest of the story is false as is much of the traditional lore about the *Somerset*. Dr. Thayer perhaps did become rich because of his practice, but a girl named Lucy was not among his treasures.

Strange and Unusual Cape Codders
In the days before social service agencies routinely intervened to make sure that everyone was "normal," Cape Cod had its share of individuals who, shall we say, were a bit "eccentric." And there were, no doubt, a number of citizens who, by any standard, probably could have stood some reform. Amos Otis, who researched some of the earliest Cape families, mentioned a few of them. On his death in October of 1875, his friends noted that Otis "was genuine, and had no patience with shams and unrealities. For him the simple truth was the utmost skill." This unwillingness to mince words probably explains why Amos Otis, with his candid style of writing, was an early practitioner of the "tell it like it is," school of journalism.

Of William Casely, an early Barnstable settler, he wrote: "Though educated, he was a vulgar man, and though a professor of religion, he did not live a Christian life. He was weak minded, vain, frivolous, and committed acts that gentlemen are ashamed to have laid to their charge. The sentence of excommunication pronounced against him was a righteous one; and though he continued to reside in Barnstable, he sunk into merited ignominy."

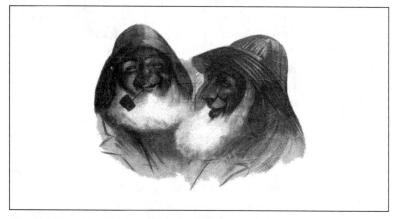

Cape Cod Characters. (Jim Coogan collection)

Otis was just as blunt in describing the life of Yarmouth's Andrew Hallett. "He was frequently a party involved in law suits ... Mr. Hallett did not recover damages in any of his law suits, and it may be inferred that he was a little stiff necked, and believed his own to be the better way, a trait of character which many of his descendants, down to the fifth generation, inherited." Receiving similar treatment was Barnstable's Samuel Bacon. "He was," wrote Otis, "A captain, a man of some property, and had the bump of self esteem largely developed." Writing about the life of Doctor Richard Bourne of Sandwich, he remarked, "He was temperate in his habits; that is, he was never intoxicated at his own expense."

He summarized Rebecca Blush's religious views by stating that, "In her religious opinions she was orthodox; and she hated the Methodists, not because they were innovators, but because the preachers called at her house, and because her husband contributed something to their support." And of Thomas Joyce of Yarmouth, Otis observed that "[He] had a large family of girls noted for their beauty, which however, did not prevent the father from committing suicide."

Odd behavior was also not overlooked by Otis. Nathaniel Coleman's strange phobia apparently didn't affect his standing in the community. "[He] was insane the latter part of his life. He believed the land everywhere had become soft and miry. He carried a very long cane with a ram's horn on the upper end, and his hat was ornamented with feathers of various colors, stuck under the band. Notwithstanding his constant fear of sinking, he was good natured, cheerful, and inoffensive."

Another character who was a bit different was Yarmouth's Nathaniel Gorham, who Otis described as "Eccentric in his habits, and in his manners ... In dress, he not only adhered to the fashions of his ancestors; but in some particulars was an oddity. He wore his shirt with the open part behind, and fastened at the back of the neck with a loop and a nail. Notwithstanding his oddities, he was industrious, honest and prudent, an obliging neighbor, and a good citizen."

Still another character who made the Otis list of unique personalities was Jonathan Lewis of Barnstable. "In traveling to Cincinnati," Otis wrote, "He carried with him a large family of small children. He lost one out of his wagon and did not miss it til he had traveled nearly a day and went back and found it."

And finally, there were the Barnstable brothers Josiah and Edward Childs. Otis remarked that, "For fourteen years subsequent to 1800, these brothers were oftener seen together than separate. Every weekday at 11 and 4 o'clock, they visited the groceries with a degree of punctuality which all noticed. Housewives that had no time pieces, when they saw them, would say, 'Uncle Ned and Siah (as they were familiarly called) have passed, and it is time to set the table.'" Interestingly, Otis reveals that toward the end of their lives the brothers had a falling out over something and never spoke to each other again.

"Road Tax" Collector
Cape Cod's history is garnished with legendary characters that lent a certain flavor to this place. Yet, few could match Barney Gould. His quirkiness and strange exploits earned him a place in the local history books ... right alongside famous sea captains and impassioned patriots, each making their unique mark upon these shores.

There was probably no one quite like Gould. Who knows for sure if the stories attached to his name are actually true, or whether these stories have been stretched over the years. Regardless, whether they are fact or folklore, it all makes for interesting tales that point to the Cape's true persona as a home to those who existed slightly off center.

Several towns claim Barney Gould. Chatham seems to have been the place of his birth but he lived the bulk of his life in the "Happy Hollow" section of Hyannis. This section, located in the west end of the village, was home to the lower class members of society at the time (including the Irish!) and earned its nickname from the "happy" nature of its sometimes-intoxicated residents. No doubt, some of its reputation was rooted in fact ... and some of that was the product of someone's interpretation of fact.

Hattie Blossom Fritze, in her book, *Horse and Buggy Days on Old Cape Cod*, described Gould as thus: "My impression is of a man, not young, of medium size and build, with a piece of cart rope tied around his middle ... I suppose the rope was used because he had lost buttons, but I never forgot how odd it looked. This must have been back in 1893." According to Fritze, Gould would "pick up a living here and there." For instance, he would deliver mail and packages in his wheelbarrow over long distances for "a few pennies," sometimes journeying as far away as Falmouth (or even Boston), hitching a ride on the train!

Gould was a great one for making wagers. He once bet a man that he could beat him to Boston even though the man was at the station about to board the next train. Of course, the crafty Gould won the bet. He rode on the cowcatcher at the front of the locomotive and arrived in Boston ahead of the rest of the train—and the wagering passenger.

Another time, Gould made a bet with a sea captain who was leaving on a journey around Cape Horn for San Francisco that he could get there first overland. Again Gould was victorious, hitchhiking across the country, according to *Cape Cod Pilot* author Josef Berger, "from one prairie schooner to another." Still another $25 bet had Gould claiming that he could get to Bermuda "without stepping off Cape Cod soil all the way." A Hyannis sea captain, who was leaving for the island that day, took the bait and sailed away believing that he couldn't possibly lose this wager. Several days later as the captain was loading cargo at Hamilton harbor, he saw a ship approaching the pier. Gould was standing on the deck of the incoming vessel. "I'm here to collect my $25," shouted Gould, as the ships closed on one another. "What do you mean?" said the sea captain. "You came here on a ship didn't you? You will be paying me." "Not so," replied Gould, "I was on Cape Cod soil all the way." The captain boarded the other ship and found Gould standing in his wheelbarrow, which was filled with Cape Cod dirt. "I never left it the whole voyage, even to sleep," said Gould. The sea captain forked over the $25.

Perhaps more than anything Gould was known as an unofficial "road tax" collector. Any time he met someone along his journeys around the Cape he demanded a road tax, typically two cents for the year. It was, essentially, panhandling with a purpose. Most people humored Gould and paid the money. Supposedly, Gould met up with a doctor one day who gave him ten cents, to which Gould remarked, "Your road tax is paid up for five years!" Another time he went into a store where a cross-eyed man was making a purchase. The man turned and stared in another direction as he greeted Barney. Being the first cross-eyed person that he had ever met, Barney was puzzled as to whether the man was really looking at him or not. Finally he asked the man, "Who are ye lookin at?" "Why you, of course," the cross-eyed man replied, "Who else?" "Well then, why don't ye look at me?" Gould asked. The man kept looking away, all the while still talking to Gould. Needless to say, the startled Gould didn't collect any road tax from that man.

Blind Frank

One of the forgotten characters of nineteenth century Cape Cod is Frank Holaday of Hyannis. Known as "Blind Frank" because he had been sightless from birth, Holaday played the fiddle with such vigor and skill that he was known from Monument Beach to Monomoy's Power Hole.

Holaday was a fixture at barn dances and harvest events and generations of young people looked forward to "hazing and setting" to the beat of his music. Some said his name should have been "Holiday" because he was always present at some celebration or other across the Cape. He would arrive at a village "hoe down" carrying his fiddle in a dirty green bag and be helped to the front of the hall where he would begin playing music that he composed himself. His favorite tunes were "Tu you can't, and tu you can," and "Off she goes to Miramashee." One observer who watched the old fiddler in action noted that when he began to play it was wise to "look sharp for heel taps in your face, from the feet of the sweating and puffing youngsters, who 'put it down' on the loose boards at his side."

Each year at the annual sheep shearing on Nantucket, Frank would arrive during the third week of June aboard "Uncle Zeke" Matthews' sloop *Lydia* out of Hyannis. It was said that he did not miss a shearing in fifty years. Wearing a blue coat with bright buttons with short waist and swallowtails, he would sit under a tent at Miacomet and play for the dancers. Whalers not at sea attended and it was said that black and white sailors danced together. "The white whaleman in his shirt sleeves, and the black one in his blouse, danced and reeled 'till the sweat poured over the thick lips of the darkey like the rushing rain drops over a roll of sole leather."

For his work, Frank would charge "six cents on the boards and three cents on the bare ground."

"To be sure," wrote a critic, "His performance was not of the most scientific kind ... But with a little 'whiteface' or 'blackstrap' to give his spirits a cheer up, he would jerk off as much music from four fiddle strings as any other live man."

When "Blind Frank" died at age 74 in 1864, he was remembered in a poem entitled, "The Harper."

> "Onward, but not unheeded went
> The Harper old; his form was bent,
> His doublet wool, his hose were tow,
> His pantaloons were cut so, so.
> The people gazed, the Coofs admired,
> And many stranger things transpired;
> Coppers from many a hand were wrung,
> As, wading through the sand he sung—
> 'Tis tu I can't and tu I can,
> All the way to Shearing pen.'

The "Foolishness" of James Knowles

As a young man, James Knowles of Eastham went to sea like most of the other boys in that town. On one voyage, he took a fall from the rigging and landed on his head. While it didn't kill him, his injuries affected him for the rest of his life. He was described by his neighbors as being "always happy, but a bit foolish."

Knowles couldn't hold any kind of a steady job after his mishap and his family began to worry about him. His brother thought that just sitting around might eventually change James's happy mood and bring him into a state of depression that he would never recover from. So he brought James some materials and suggested that he might build himself a small boat for shellfishing. James took to the idea with enthusiasm and for most of the winter he could be seen heading down to the harbor, lugging materials back and forth from the family farm. In May, he announced to his family that his boat was about ready to be launched and that on the following Saturday they could all come to the harbor to witness the event.

When the day came, the family was assembled at the water's edge to see the launching of a nicely built 18-foot skiff. James pushed his newly completed craft into the water where it promptly sank. Puzzled as to why a brand new boat would sink so quickly, the family moved closer to inspect the craft. They discovered that the afternoon before, when James had finished the final work on his boat, he had bored a good size hole in the bottom to brush out all of the left over shavings!

The Wellfleet Oysterman

When Henry David Thoreau came to Cape Cod in the middle of the nineteenth century, he was intent on studying both the natural and the social landscape of the place. His observations about some of the people he met during his four trips to the Cape were not always flattering. He did not sugarcoat his characters, revealing their personalities, warts and all. Above all, he enjoyed sitting and talking with real people. On one occasion, he and his traveling companion, William Ellery Channing, stayed a night at the home of John Young Newcomb on Williams Pond in Wellfleet. The old man was almost into his nineties and became the famous Wellfleet Oysterman in Thoreau's classic book, *Cape Cod*.

Newcomb entertained his two visitors with tales of a long life. He told them that as a teenager he had heard the sound of cannons firing across the bay from the battle of Bunker Hill. He claimed to have seen George Washington riding his horse through the streets of Boston. He told them that he had sailed around the world in his youth but wasn't long on specifics. A plain talking man, Newcomb conversed in non-stop fashion on topics from religion to the kinds of plants that were in his garden. He talked of recent shipwrecks that he had witnessed. At one point, the old man's wife, who Thoreau characterized as having a "hardness and coarseness that no man ever possesses or suggests," finally had to remind her husband that, with his enthusiasm for conversation, he'd stayed up well past his bedtime. Thoreau noted that when the old man prepared for bed, he exhibited legs, "as fair and plump as an infant's."

Newcomb admitted to his visitors that his ability to control his own household had been largely unsuccessful. And he allowed that he was pretty much resigned to his fate. "I am a poor, good for nothing crittur, as Isaiah says: I am all broken down this year. I am under petticoat government here." He added that he saw his elderly wife and the daughter that lived with them also as "good for nothing critturs."

After a night in the old house, and a breakfast of eels, buttermilk cake, cold bread, green beans, donuts, and tea, Thoreau and Channing made ready to depart. The old oysterman seemed reluctant to let them leave, following them outside and continuing an animated conversation across his half-acre garden plot. Finally, with a wave, he pointed across the fields toward the sound of the ocean. As if using the older man's stance as a compass, the two younger men headed east toward the Great Beach.

Chapter 4

Out to Sea

Much of Cape Cod's past can be found upon the rising and falling ocean waves. Whether sailing on local waters upon the village packet or far away from home upon a clipper ship, stories abound of Cape Codders at sea.

Barnstable's Shipyards

The area's long history of constructing sailing vessels dates back to the time of the Pilgrims and the first vessel built in Plimoth Colony. Described as a pinnace, or a small sailboat, it was built in 1627 at the Pilgrims' trading post at Manomet (Bourne).

The earliest settlers on the Cape were farmers, but eventually they took to the sea. And so, down to the sea in ships went the heartiest of young men, many of them sailing on vessels built locally. First boat building in the area consisted of amateur efforts during the 17th century. If a local fisherman possessed carpentry skills he might construct a boat for his own needs. But soon, the need outpaced the supply.

Thomas Agrey of mid-18th century Barnstable is regarded as the Cape's first professional shipbuilder, eventually teaching a number of locals his craft. Though he married a local woman (Anna Dimmick of Barnstable), the Agrey family moved away to Maine.

Typically, the Cape's first shipyards were small, specializing in sloops and schooners under 100 feet in length and catering to the local fishing and packet trades. Yards were established along a number of Cape creeks, coves, and harbors. Barnstable shipyards alone launched some 50 vessels during the first part of the 19th century. Hyannis shipbuilders included Watson Holmes, Abner Lovell, Richard Lewis, Gorham Lovell, and brothers Walter and Benjamin

Carney, while Barnstable village had Josiah Lewis and Charles Dimmock, the latter built vessels at Rendezvous Creek. Between 1820 and 1840, William Lewis built a number of vessels to the east at Maraspin Creek, including the 186-ton brig *Cummaquid*. Osterville's Oliver Hinckley and Seth Goodspeed were active at East Bay, with Hinckley building more than 20 vessels between 1817 and 1845, most of them schooners. And not to be outdone, Cotuit had shipbuilders Job Handy and James Coleman.

The nearby village of Centerville saw its first shipbuilder in the person of Jesse Crosby, a Revolutionary War veteran. Eventually, the village would boast two shipyards—one located at Centerville Harbor and another at Craigville Beach. The harbor operation, which would see more than 30 vessels built between 1824 and 1860, was run by James Crosby, Jonathan Kelley, and Deacon Samuel Crosby. Of these, most were light tonnage coasting vessels used to transport cargoes along the northeast coast. By the mid-1820's Kelley was building sloops and schooners, typically producing two per year. Meanwhile, at Craigville Beach, the Centerville Wharf Company began operations in the 1850's, specializing in larger 200-ton vessels. Besides the shipyard, there was also a wharf that served as a port and housed various ship-related businesses. Items received at the port were assessed a tariff, such as two cents for a bag of coffee, two cents for a barrel of flour, one cent for a keg of nails, or even 12 cents for a cord of wood. Yet, shipbuilding remained the core business, with new vessels fetching up to $40,000 for a three-masted schooner. Though the company survived the Civil War years that saw other shipyards on Cape close down, the Centerville Wharf Company was eventually closed in 1879.

A different kind of boat was being built in Osterville during the 19th century. The catboat was a relatively small, sturdy vessel developed by the descendants of Centerville shipbuilder Jesse Crosby. It's believed that sometime between 1845 and 1850 brothers Horace and Worthington Crosby built *Little Eva*—the very first catboat. It's further believed that the brothers obtained their plans for the new boat design via a séance—from their deceased shipbuilder father, Andrew.

Communication with the spirit world was all the rage at the time, and the Crosby brothers' mother considered herself a spiritual medium. Apparently she communicated regularly with her deceased husband and was able to garner key information that helped the brothers construct their new craft.

The naming of the first catboat, though, is a bit of a mystery. "Eva" may have taken her name from the Bible's Eve, or perhaps the character from the book *Uncle Tom's Cabin*, which was printed around that same time. And one cannot rule out that perhaps Eva was a local girl that caught the eye of one of the Crosby brothers.

As for the term "catboat," the vessel was so-named because it was said to turn as "quick as a cat." Early catboats were built of oak and cedar; later boats were crafted from mahogany, cypress, and even spruce. They ranged between 12 and 25 feet in length with a design that was unusually wide in the beam. A gaff-rigged sail was situated in the front section of the boat. Overall, its design rendered it quite seaworthy and allowed for easy maneuverability. It quickly became popular with local fishermen and those who moved small cargoes along the coast.

Soon, a number of Crosbys were building catboats. According to the *Barnstable Directory of 1895*—sort of a 19th century version of the Yellow Pages—Herbert F. Crosby manufactured "all kinds of pleasure boats," including the "celebrated Crosby Cabin Cat Boats." His directory listing goes on to read, "These boats are noted for their staunchness, speed and comfort." Also included in the directory are boat builders Daniel Crosby, Charles Crosby, and Wilton Crosby. H. Manley Crosby is listed as a builder of "yachts of all kind up to 60 feet in length."

The early 20th century saw the Crosbys of Osterville building sloops, which were dubbed Wianno Senior and Wianno Junior. A reward was offered to any sailor who could manage to tip over a Wianno Senior. At first popular fishing boats, the Wianno series became even more popular leisure boats during the roaring 1920s. One of the most celebrated of these crafts was the *Victura* out of Hyannisport, which belonged to President John F. Kennedy.

Figureheads—From "Old Ironsides" to "Old Hickory"
Upon a wide and deep ocean, a man is like a speck of kelp drifting at the whim of the waves. Mariners who ventured into this unforgiving realm were quite aware of their place in the scope of the

seas, and were thankful for every successful voyage that landed them back on the sandy shores of home. As such, superstitious indeed were the seafarers of centuries ago as they bargained with Poseidon for their souls. And one piece of their superstition revolved around the figurehead that graced the bow of their ship.

Figureheads date back thousands of years to the first seafarers who believed that only with the gods' help would they return from their voyages. Ancient Egyptians, Greeks, Phoenicians, and even Romans affixed figureheads to their vessels in an attempt to control the outcome of their nautical exploits. These figureheads were religious in nature and were used to appease a particular god who might watch over their voyages by calming the waves, producing a needed wind, or even bringing victory in battle.

Situated at the bow, the figurehead was believed to watch ahead for danger, as if the very eyes of the ship. Typically, figureheads of long ago were some form of beast with its gaze fixed on the horizon. The image of the figurehead also provided the vessel with a persona, giving life to the inanimate wooden hulk. By making the vessel a "living, breathing creature," it was believed that the ship would react to oncoming danger as an animal in the wild might react.

Beasts and dragons graced Norse vessels of a thousand or more years ago. With the spread of Christianity, European ships began to display religious images at the bow such as saints or even the Virgin Mary in Catholic countries. For a time just prior to the Renaissance, figureheads were no longer in vogue, yet they were reintroduced in the 16th century with improved ship designs that featured a "beak" bow. Elaborate figureheads began to take their place on the bows of ships, along with ornate scrolling. Lions and kings sailed at the front of British vessels, their imposing images meant to lead the crew to victory at sea. Warring nations battled on the figurehead front in an attempt to outdo its foe. In one battle a British ship displayed a figurehead in the form of a skeleton, with the opposing French vessel carrying a corpse figurehead.

American ships also carried figureheads. Perhaps the most popular to grace the bowsprit of Cape vessels was that of a woman, representing all the women that the crew might dream of—wife, mother, lover, the girl next door, or even the lass who serves pints at the local tavern. Regardless, upon a long journey the figurehead of a woman provided comfort for lonesome crewmen. Such feminine figures, whether saintly or seductive, lent a maternal accompaniment to the voyage.

But not all local vessels wore feminine figureheads. The nineteenth century American warship *USS Constitution*, when built at Boston in 1798, sported a figurehead of Hercules at her bow. This figure was most likely chosen to project an image of strength and courage as "Old Ironsides" was constructed with an eye on possible war with France. Yet, figureheads can be fleeting, and around 1807 the warship carried an image of Neptune. By the 1830s, the figurehead of "Old Ironsides" was changed again, to that of President Andrew Jackson.

A figurehead controversy involved Cape Cod sea captain Josiah Richardson and the vessel under his command—*Staffordshire*. Launched in 1852, the *Staffordshire* sported a figurehead in the form of a white witch, which caused the clairvoyant Fox sisters of Arcadia, New York to predict doom for the vessel and those who sailed upon her. As a result of the publicity, the maiden voyage of the vessel was delayed by a week.

Staffordshire reached San Francisco in 101 days, breaking a number of sailing ship speed records and debunking the Fox sister's earlier predictions. Yet doom did visit the vessel during the following year when she wrecked off Nova Scotia in a storm and sank along with 175 passengers and crew, including Captain Richardson.

The Beheading of Andrew Jackson

In the early summer of 1834, fresh from a refit, the storied warship *U.S.S. Constitution* was back in Boston. She was about to leave on a three-year mission to the Mediterranean to promote American interests in the region. Her commander, Jesse Duncan Elliot, was new to "Old Ironsides," and during the ship's overhaul he made a change that infuriated the city.

Elliot was a staunch Jacksonian Democrat and he replaced the old ship's figurehead with a likeness of the seventh President. It was a full size image of "Old Hickory," a wide brimmed hat held in his left hand. While one might think that this was a proper thing to do to honor the nation's chief executive, it was like waving a red flag in front of the staunchly Whig city. The majority of the citizens of Boston were outraged but there wasn't much they could do about it. The Navy had a right to put just about anything they wanted on their vessels and it was hard to argue that a likeness of the President of the United States was inappropriate.

But there was someone who was determined to do something about the affront and it was Captain Samuel Worthington Dewey of Falmouth. Recently returned from a voyage to the West Indies in his brig *Falcon*, Dewey was having dinner with his ship's owners, the Lincoln brothers—William and Henry, also of Falmouth. When the subject got around to how the *Constitution* had been desecrated by the new figurehead, Dewey said that he was of a mind to row out to the ship and cut Jackson's head clean off. Egged on by his

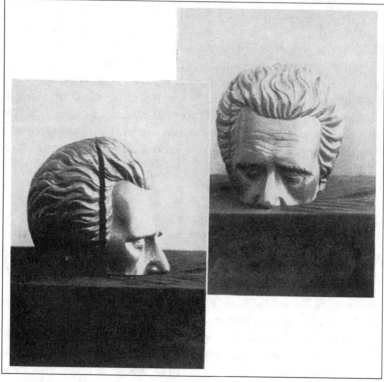

Andrew Jackson's Severed Head. (Cape Cod Community College)

friends and the promise of a $100 payment if he could pull it off, Dewey began to put together his plan to decapitate Andrew Jackson. Observing the warship for several days, Captain Dewey made himself familiar with the ship's routine. He noted when the watch changed and how the sentries reacted to weather changes. Having evaluated the ship's vulnerabilities, he was convinced that he could carry out his plan.

On a rainy night in July with the clouds pouring torrents into Boston Harbor and thunder rumbling, Dewey rowed a small dory out to the *Constitution*. He found a rope hanging down from the main deck and under the cover of the cloudburst he climbed up the side of the ship. Once aboard, he timed the Marine Guard's movement and then got himself to the bow. Lowering himself just below the bowsprit, he began to saw the head off the figurehead, his cutting noises masked by the rainstorm. Cutting through the image just below the nose, Dewey was able to sever the upper portion of the head from the body. Carrying his prize in a sack, and praying that the storm would continue to give him cover, Dewey retraced his steps to his small boat and rowed safely to shore where he hid his prize in a nearby woodshed.

The next day, when the deed was revealed, Captain Elliot was fit to be tied. He offered a $1,000 reward for the return of the head and for the apprehension of the person who had cut it off. Democratic newspapers howled in protest, noting that "this act was done by some vile scoundrel, of whose neck, the halter has too long been cheated." At this point, Captain Dewey was probably a bit sobered as to the seriousness of his act. So he made sure that the head left his possession and was transferred to some of the more prominent Whig politicians in the city. He collected his $100 and kept quiet about his role in the affair.

Andrew Jackson's severed head became an object of mirth and political commentary. It became a "trophy," circulated and exhibited at Whig party dinners. The head made its way to New York and then to Philadelphia. At one point it served as a centerpiece, almost like the head of John the Baptist, at a party fundraiser at the Astor Hotel in New York City presided over by Daniel Webster.

When the *Constitution* sailed for her Mediterranean duty station in July of 1834, she sported a new Andrew Jackson figurehead paid for by Captain Elliot. As for the severed head, it was eventually returned years later to the Navy Department, some say by Dewey himself. Apparently his Yankee conscience got the best of him and he felt he had to make a "clean breast" of things.

The Local Packet
Before the railroad came to Cape Cod, and before steamships became popular, sailing vessels known as packets were the preferred method of moving cargoes from port to port. These vessels provided an important means of connecting local Cape communities with various east coast cities.

Romantic images of the packet were captured in ink by early 20th century Cape writer Joseph Lincoln, in his book *Cape Cod Yesterdays:*

"A fair day in summer and we can imagine a sail out and across Cape Cod Bay. The sky blue and clear; the yellow and white sand of the beaches shining in the sunshine; the water green, until we cross the outer bar, and then blue with white trimmings; the distant village showing its roofs above the edging of pines and elms, with the green salt marshes for a foreground; the little schooner heeling a bit in the fresh breeze ..."

Yarmouth and Boston.

Packet schooner NORTH will commence running between Yarmouth and Boston the first opportunity after the 1st of March next. Terms for freight, reasonable. Superior accommodations for passengers. Small packages must be settled for on delivery.

Orders sent in care of H. C. Thacher, 13 Central Wharf, or Winslow & Myrick, or E. & F. King, Boston, will meet with prompt attention.

EDWARD GORHAM, Master.

Feb. 26, 1864.

Sailing Notice for the Yarmouth Packet. (Cape Cod Community College)

And yet, Lincoln also tells of another side of packet travel, touching on the extremes, from the doldrums and bouts of seasickness to the "howling northeast gale." According to the author: "The packets are pleasant to read about and chat about, but as a regular means of travel, I am certain I should have preferred the stagecoach with its stops at the taverns."

Throughout much of the 19th century, local packets moved various cargoes, the US mail, and passengers between ports. Cargoes could include sea salt, cranberries, cod, mackerel, or even locally grown turnips. This saltwater connection provided a valuable commercial link with merchants in the larger cities. Many local sloops and schooners made the run between Cape Cod and Boston as well as to other northeast ports. Yarmouth had a number of vessels—*Commodore Hull, Emerald, H.S. Barnes*, and the aptly named *Yarmouth*. North side packets typically sailed to Boston; south side packets to New York and New Jersey. A packet might sail up to three times a week, with roundtrip passage between a Cape port and Boston typically running less than two dollars.

The local village packet was a source of great pride. Every village claimed to have the fastest vessel. Wagers were made between residents of neighboring towns as captains prepared their vessels for races to Boston. Early 20th century author Henry Kittredge makes mention of a race between the Yarmouth sloop, *Commodore Hull*, and the sloop *Mail*, out of Barnstable. At the time—the 1840's—the *Commodore Hull* was deemed the fastest packet on Cape Cod, so two Barnstable sea captains (named Hinckley and Percival) built the *Mail* to defeat the Yarmouth packet. Their efforts were not in vain as the Barnstable packet edged out the Yarmouth vessel by three lengths.

Eventually, the age of the packet came to a close, their demise brought about by the coming of the railroad and a rapid decline in the salt making industry. And alas, no longer did the packets race for Beantown.

A Sailor's Letter Home

Cape Codders started to experience long family separations as sailors began to trade up and down the Atlantic coast in the 18th century. The emerging coasting trade saw sloops and schooners hauling raw materials from the southern states and returning again to places like Charleston, South Carolina and Savannah, Georgia with finished goods from New England. Salted fish was shipped to the Caribbean islands and Cuba to feed plantation workers and molasses was carried back north to be distilled into rum for export to Europe and Africa.

Cape skippers soon became familiar with rivers and harbors from the Chesapeake to the Carolinas. Boston became a leading port and the foundations of later 19th century maritime fortunes were laid in that city. Sailors did the best they could to keep in touch with loved ones back home, dashing off a letter and sending it on a ship bound for Cape Cod. Not much correspondence survives from those early days but one piece that did is a short letter that a Brewster sailor wrote to his younger sister while his ship was in Baltimore. Across more than two centuries it still rings with a sense of concern that often marks the brother and sister relationships.

The letter is transcribed and reproduced with its misspellings and formalized style. Despite its antiquated language, the sentiments and advice could well have been written yesterday.

Baltimore August ye 31, 1789

Dear Sister,
I have now an opportunity to answer your elegant letter of June ye first. But I must beg your pardon before I proceade any further for not being aquainted with so much elegancy as your pen: I shall forme but a ruff epistle: But I have no reason to think but that you will grant it as you know I am but a poor saler and was never capible to improve in that line of bisnes:
Phebe, you very much surprise me when you talk of being an oald made before you have past the teens. But I might make sum alowance for your seeing so many oald mades, and I may add oalder girls around you: ... and I haven't reson to believe it as cuz of your fair complexion over spread with such a glow of helth can't fail to captivate the harts of sum of the younger bachilers: But Dear Sister you make to many apologise for the hat I sent you which I think was not worth mentioning but I fancy [if] you are afraid of emptying my purse (which by the way is almost worn out) then you must be my Depter to send for me a note of hand [conveying] my love to Miss Desire Foster and I thank her for her respectful compliment

and I should be happy to serve her in any respect and wish it might be on a voyage of mattrimona as I fancy we should sail very pleasantly through life. My best respects to her mamma and to her much admired sister Lydia.

Phebe I hope this will find you all in good helth as it leaves me. And I beg you may command me when you think I can in the least serve you, for I am your faithful and affectionate brother,
Lot Clark

It is probable that seaman Clark carried the letter to another New England bound vessel for transfer to Phebe who likely received it some time in September of 1789. A close inspection of the worn parchment has a curious penciled notation near the bottom—clearly written in another hand, "Lost at sea." A check of family records reveals that this, indeed, was the case. As Lot Clark's ship was returning from the Chesapeake Bay bound for Providence, Rhode Island, he and the rest of his mates were lost in a late November gale. Phebe never saw her brother again. He was 26 years old. She later married Benjamin Gage in March of 1793. He died on a voyage to the West Indies less than a year later. At the age of 24, Phebe Clark became a widow and an "oald made"

Some Sea Captains of Yarmouth Port
Drive the winding and picturesque Route 6A in Yarmouth Port and you are riding past history. Many of the houses that line the old carriage route are the former homes of sea captains; their floorboards tread by the shoes of men that plied the oceans of the world.

For instance, the Captain Bangs Hallet House on Strawberry Lane was built in the 1840's (actually, from a smaller house on the property dating to the mid-1700's). Owned by the Thacher family, the house was sold to a Captain Allen Knowles of the village. During the same period, Captain Hallet owned a house further west along the road. The two sea captains were good friends, and when time came to retire they decided to swap houses, so Hallet and his wife Anna relocated to Strawberry Lane. Perhaps there was a reason why the Hallets decided to move from their previous house, as Death knocked many times on their door. Between 1837 and 1852 they endured the loss of two infant sons, three infant daughters, and a three-year old daughter. Captain Hallet and his wife remained at the Strawberry Lane house until their own deaths in the 1890's. (The Greek revival style house serves today as the home of the Historical Society of Old Yarmouth.)

During the middle decades of the 19th century, Captain Hallet was engaged in the China-India trade. For a time, he served as master of the vessel *Herbert*, aboard which young Cape Cod men learned the ways of the sea. One of these lads who grew up "before the mast" was mate William Burgess of Brewster. Hallet apparently had a great deal of confidence in Burgess for when the esteemed sea captain took a brief vacation from the sea he recommended Burgess as master for a voyage to Calcutta. At the voyage's conclusion, Burgess handed the reins of the *Herbert* back "to her former and able Commander, Bangs Hallet, Esq., wishing her pleasant and successful voyages."

Successful voyages were Hallet's good fortune throughout his career. One such voyage, according to a passenger list published in an edition of the *Boston Daily Evening Transcript* in 1853, saw wife Anna accompany the captain to San Francisco.

For a number of Cape families, the sea was a common thread that ran from one brother to another. A younger brother would follow his older brother to sea, perhaps each rising up through the ranks to become master of his own sailing ship. One Yarmouth example is that of the Eldridge brothers—Asa, John, and Oliver.

Every Cape history book worth its salt mentions Asa Eldridge as a sea captain who set a longstanding sailing ship record with a 13-day, one hour and 25 minute Atlantic crossing as master of the clipper *Red Jacket* in 1854. His seafaring days ended two years later, though, when his latest command—the 280-foot steamer *Pacific*—mysteriously sank with no survivors upon an Atlantic crossing (most likely her boiler blew up, which was a common danger among steamships of that age). Perhaps Captain Asa should have stuck to canvas.

Though Asa's exploits earned him a place in the history books, his two, lesser-known brothers deserve mention as well. The eldest brother, John, commanded the Swallow Tail Line's vessel *Liverpool* in the 1840's, with youngest brother Oliver serving as mate. In his book *The Shipmasters of Cape Cod*, Henry Kittredge described John as "a Herculean figure even among the hardy brotherhood of the

Western Ocean … With the head and brow of a Gladstone and the physique of a professional wrestler." One legend states that he clean-jerked an "1,800-pound hogshead of tobacco." In another story, while in a southern port, he single-handedly took on a "gang of thugs." Apparently, he hoisted the ringleader over his head and carried him to the local police authorities. Later, during the Civil War, he served as commander of a troop ship, the Collins Line's *Baltic*, which had been converted for war duty.

Youngest brother Oliver eventually stepped out from beneath John's shadow to become a master mariner, sailing throughout the Pacific in the China trade. In the 1850's he was captain of the clipper *Titan*, and during the war years of the 1860's he was placed in command of the *Atlantic*, another Naval employed Collins vessel. After the war, he took a position with the Pacific Mail Company, eventually becoming president of a number of west coast companies (primarily in natural gas, telephone, and insurance).

Another brotherhood of Yarmouth Port sea captains could be found in the brothers Mathews—Oliver, Samuel Jr., Nathaniel, and Richard. Master of the brig *Isabel*, Oliver retired early from the sea due to illness. His two-story Georgian style three-quarter home located along 6A was built in 1835. Here he lived for half a century with his wife Phebe. The captain's remains rest in a family plot at the Center Street cemetery, where also lie brothers Samuel and Nathaniel. Testament to the hard times of the 19th century are the stones of two of Oliver and Phebe's sons who died very young— one at age ten months and another at just three days.

The Queen and Captain Nye

Though Sandwich lacked an adequate harbor during the great age of sail, the town was able to produce one of the Cape's great sea captains. In fact, he was once even recognized by the Queen of England.

Captain Ezra Nye set speed records under both sail and steam. As a sea master of the Liverpool packet trade, his first speedy passage was aboard the *Amethyst*. In 1829, he sailed her across the Atlantic in a stingy twenty days. News of his success spread through the seafaring community and as a result more prestigious commands were offered to him.

Throughout the 1830's he was captain of the packet *Independence*, on which he continued to prove himself a first rate master mariner. Once, he made the round trip voyage between Liverpool and New York City in just 34 days. Some of his sailing ship records remained unbroken until the coming of the clipper ships.

In the 1850's, Nye made the jump from sail to steam to command the *Pacific* of the Collins Line. He swiftly delivered a nine-day, twenty-hour Atlantic passage, becoming the first sea captain to make the ocean crossing in under ten days.

But speed, however, was not the only thing for which Captain Nye was known. He also proved himself an honorable sea master who followed the code of the seas. Queen Victoria once awarded him a gold chronometer as a token of thanks for his efforts in saving the passengers and crewmembers of the *Jesse Stephens*, a wrecked British vessel.

Chapter 5

Hardship on the Oceans

With ocean voyages came ocean hardships. Cape Codders were no strangers to shipwreck, scurvy, starvation, yellow fever, kidnapping, pirate attacks, Confederate attacks, and even being swallowed by a whale!

Scurvy on the High Seas

During the age of sail, ships could be at sea for months or even the better part of a year before making landfall. While at sea, the crew survived off whatever foods they had in the ship's store. Traditionally, such food consisted of smoked fish, meats, and grains, all washed down with a quaff of grog. Of course, fresh caught fish was also on the menu.

Normally absent from the menu, though, were adequate portions of vegetables and fruits. In this era before refrigeration, it was an impossible task to keep such healthy foods from spoiling. Unfortunately, this was quite a major problem for those at sea, because without vegetables and fruits for a period of time mariners could suffer from a disease called scurvy.

Scurvy is caused by a deficiency in Vitamin C over a prolonged period, usually six months. Inflicting major damage to bones, tendons, and ligaments, this disease if allowed to progress usually resulted in death.

The first recorded shipwreck along the Cape shore involved the vessel *Sparrowhawk*, which came to woe off Nauset Beach in December 1626. This shipwreck was most likely the direct result of scurvy as well as other issues traceable to a lack of nutritional foods. The ship's captain was ill with scurvy and as such was confined to his cot for a number of days leading up to the

Sparrowhawk's encounter with the Cape coastline. Adding to the problem was the fact that the passengers and crew were out of beer (a popular beverage in that day) and the supply of drinking water was low. With an ill captain, and supplies running out, attention apparently strayed as the crew forced their vessel closer to shore in an attempt to locate a safe landing spot. Though the bars of Nauset snatched *Sparrowhawk*, fortunately all on board survived the wreck.

Mariners learned the importance of fruits and vegetables on long voyages and methods were developed to assure that these foods were made available. A local solution was found in the native cranberry growing in bogs throughout Southeastern Massachusetts. Juices made from oranges, lemons, and limes were brought along as well as baked pies containing fruit. Another solution was storing dried fruit and making planned visits to islands along the voyage in order to stock up on valuable food items.

Shriveled Bacon

The town of Barnstable produced many worthy shipmasters, such as Captain Daniel Bacon. Like many of that age, he first went to sea as a teenager, growing up before the mast.

As the years went by, he was awarded the position of first mate aboard the *Xenophon*, making the Liverpool run. In his early 20's he became the ship's master when her captain retired. Yet, the Embargo Act of 1807 grounded American shipping, including the *Xenophon*. So Bacon forfeited his command position to take a first mate position on the *Atahualpa* under the command of Captain William Sturgis. This decision would send Bacon on a three-year voyage to the orient, during which the vessel was attacked by pirates.

After two further voyages to China, Bacon was given command of the vessel *Packet* for a voyage to the Pacific Northwest for furs. Then it was on to Canton, China for tea and silk before returning home again. The War of 1812 was raging and a British blockade threatened to keep the *Packet* in Canton. Yet, Bacon managed to slip past the blockade at night and slowly make his way back to America. He was forever on the lookout for the British who might seize his vessel and impress his crew. It was not until near the end of 1815, almost a year after the end of hostilities, when the *Packet* finally returned to her homeport of Boston.

Over those harrowing couple of years Bacon had shriveled to a ghost of his former self. He had lost some 35 pounds due to the stress he endured while sailing in unfriendly waters, always watching for British ships. Once back home, Bacon's weight returned to normal and he would go on to make more voyages to the orient.

A Fiji Island Massacre

As Cape Cod whaling masters sailed into the Pacific Ocean in the 1830's, they were entering a part of the world that was virtually unknown. This was particularly true of the island cultures that the whalers encountered there. It was never a sure bet that a meeting between natives and sailors would be friendly. To be shipwrecked in some of the more remote island chains could mean a slow death by starvation or a quick and painful end at the hands of cannibals. In a number of cases, whaleships and their crews were overtaken and killed or captured by islanders. One such encounter took place in October of 1835 at Barings Island in the Fiji chain and it involved the Falmouth whale ship *Awashonks*.

The *Awashonks* was typical of most of the pre-Civil War whalers. The ship had been built just three years earlier in Falmouth at Woods Hole and was one of several launched from that place in that period. Commanded by Nantucket-born Captain Prince Coffin, the ship was about 100 feet in length and carried a crew of about 30 men.

Two years out, the vessel was making her way through the Fiji Islands. Passing one of them, some natives were seen on the shore. The captain decided to attempt to trade for fresh water and fruits. The *Awashonks* hove to about a half mile off the beach and the natives manned their dug out canoes to come out to the ship. About five small boats closed on the whaler and held up breadfruit and yams. Captain Coffin let a few of the natives on deck to trade. While this was not that unusual and, in fact, was a fairly common practice in much of the Pacific whaling areas, in this case, the decision proved to be a fateful one.

The natives seemed well enough behaved and rather child-like. They were fascinated by the ship's whaling tools—especially the long handled flensing knives that were used by the whalemen to carve the blubber into manageable sized pieces for boiling. Captain Coffin took one out to show them how it was used. Suddenly the natives moved toward the racks of flensing knives. Almost as if a plan had existed, several grabbed the sharp instruments and began to swing them at the crew. In the first moments of the action, Captain Coffin and his first mate were slain. Before the rest of the whalemen could react, the natives killed another four and took control of the deck. More canoes were seen coming from the shore. The surviving crewmembers were driven either up into the rigging or over the side.

Third mate Silas Jones had survived the initial assault and he ran forward and jumped into the forehold of the ship, pulling the hatch secure behind him. There he found several other men who had taken refuge. A few were severely wounded. Jones knew that the ship's muskets were locked in the aft of the vessel. With another man, he made his way below decks toward the Captain's cabin where he located several muskets, some ammunition, and two pistols.

Jones and his comrades began firing buckshot at the natives through open ports in the stern. Some were driven off, but many remained on the main deck, shouting and singing chants of victory. The whaleship, which had never come to anchor, was drifting toward the shore and Jones knew that once aground, they would be at the complete mercy of the natives. Prospects of survival were not good.

As his shipmates helped load the muskets, Jones and another man directed fire at the natives on deck by shooting up through the overhead. At one point, a lucky shot killed one of the native leaders as he stood near the abandoned helm. The islanders, seeing this, grabbed what they could and beat a hasty retreat into their boats.

When Jones and his mates were able to get up on deck, they encountered a scene of grisly carnage. While the wounded were being cared for, it was learned that the second mate had been driven overboard and had apparently drowned. Silas Jones, just twenty-one years old, was now in command of the *Awashonks*.

Making what repairs were necessary, Jones divided the fit members of the crew into two watch sections and set sail for the Hawaiian Islands. With only about half of the men able to assume shipboard duties, there was considerable doubt that they would reach their destination. Charts were not accurate and they sailed close to a number of islands where natives attempted to block their passage. After almost two months, on November 25, 1835, the *Awashonks* entered Honolulu. Acting Captain Jones turned the vessel over to American authorities there. When offered command of the *Awashonks*, he declined, saying that another more seasoned officer should be appointed. He served as mate for the return trip to Cape Cod.

Word of Silas Jones' quick action and resourcefulness reached his home and soon after his return to Falmouth he had several offers of command. He was named master of the Falmouth whaler *Hobomock*. Jones continued as a successful skipper for over thirty years, retiring from the sea in the mid-1860's. A respected and admired member of the community, he later served as a selectman, town moderator, and as a state legislator. In 1881 he was named as president of the Falmouth National Bank. He died in Falmouth in 1888.

The Castaway Who Would be King—and Was!

When Daniel Defoe wrote his book *Robinson Crusoe*, he may have had Brewster's John Higgins in mind. Like Crusoe, Higgins was cast up on a remote Pacific island after his ship was wrecked. But instead of just a single "Friday" to share his island life, Higgins wound up with enough companions to handle every day of the week and then some.

News of the 1849 California gold strike made many adventure seekers decide that they wanted a crack at the riches that supposedly abounded in the Golden State. One of those individuals was 18-year old John Adams Higgins, a humble sailor from Brewster. In 1850 he shipped aboard Captain Winslow Knowles' clipper ship *Albatross* and headed around the horn to San Francisco. After a few unproductive months of working the gold fields along the Sacramento River, Higgins signed on as a crewman aboard the Australia-bound steamer, *Monumental City*. Once in the "land down under," he tried various unsuccessful schemes to make his fortune. He bought a small schooner and took to cruising some of the Pacific islands in the Caroline and Marshall chains. In 1854, his small vessel was wrecked in a tropical storm. He was the only survivor.

Barely alive, Higgins drifted onto the shore of a small atoll. This island in the eastern Carolines, which goes by two names, Mokil and Wellington's island, was inhabited by about 150 natives. They had never seen a white man before. Instead of eating Higgins, as might have been his fate had he perhaps fetched up in the Fiji Islands, the natives nursed the young man back to health. In a short time, Higgins became the chief's right hand man, helping the tribe set up a trading post to supply the increasing number of visiting whaling ships with fruits and fresh water. When the chief died, the natives elected Higgins as their new leader.

Higgins reportedly took at least two wives and settled in to run a trading outfit to supply the whaling ships that came through the area. He created a comfortable and well paying situation for himself, raising and selling hogs, chickens, making coconut oil, and gathering tortoise shells. Passing missionaries mentioned that he was doing a good job of Christianizing the natives in his little kingdom. When Brewster shipmaster Charles Freeman of the whale ship *Tybee* happened to stop at the island in 1857, he was amazed to find one of his former townsmen in prosperous authority there. Freeman reportedly tried to encourage Higgins to return to Cape Cod. Higgins told Freeman that he was perfectly happy in his situation, thank you. But at least word eventually got back to his family members in Brewster that he was still alive.

Two years later, in 1859, when the New Bedford whaler *Florida* stopped at Mokil, the wife of the ship's captain wasn't very charitable in her description of Higgins' lifestyle. In her view, he had descended to the level of a savage. But she did comment that his house was neat and that his two young boys were very polite. The captain of the *Florida* convinced Higgins to sail to New Zealand with them. The "Island King" took one of his sons aboard the *Florida* and made the trip to Auckland.

Some months later, deciding that he preferred his self-imposed exile, Higgins returned to Mokil but found that another man had taken his place on the island as chief. He moved once more, this time settling on nearby Pingelap Island where he apparently also became king and where he continued as a trader.

There are two accounts of the eventual fate of John Higgins. His brother, George W. Higgins, longtime Brewster postmaster, claimed that sometime in 1861 or 1862 natives from a nearby island came to Pingelap and got into a fight with some of Higgins' people. During his attempt to stop the fighting, Higgins was reportedly stabbed by one of the intruders and killed. Higgins' brother said that in retaliation, the killer was hunted down and butchered by the distraught subjects of the fallen Cape Codder. "His own people," wrote George Higgins, "were so enraged that they tore the intruders limb from limb, and then cast them into the sea for the sharks, which, according to one of their superstitions, is the most dreadful thing that can happen to one, dead or alive, as it means no future life for them."

Another account of what happened to John Higgins comes from George Westbrook, a young Englishman who arrived in the Caroline Islands about 1870. "Love of the bottle was the most over-whelming sin of the many to which this member of the Higgins clan was heir," wrote Westbrook of what was being said about the late island king. "He was a great toper. But alcohol changed him from a friendly, warm hearted man to a fiend. He was capable of any sudden frenzy while in his cups." According to Westbrook, it was in one of these drunken frenzies that Higgins died violently in a brawl in the fall of 1861, when he got into a fight with a native and was stabbed to death.

A final piece of information supplied by George Westbrook tells of a white European who had apparently known Higgins and who arrived on Pingelap several weeks after Higgins' death. The natives were suspicious of this man and they caught him one night attempting to dig up Higgins' body to get a valuable ring that Higgins always wore. The natives killed the European and reburied the body of their white chief, and in Westbrook's words, "to this day the ring circles a finger sealed to dust in the heart of a lonely coral isle."

Higgins' effects were packed up and put aboard a New Bedford whaleship to be sent home to his family in Brewster, but they never arrived. All of his cash and valuables—an amount, according to his brother, worth something like $20,000—were stolen by the ship's crew.

Saved by a Pocket Watch
Benjamin F. Bourne of Sandwich was serving as a mate aboard the
New Bedford schooner *John Allyne* when, in 1849, while rounding
Cape Horn on a voyage to California, he was taken hostage by
natives. The circumstances of his capture and eventual escape
became the subject of a book that he wrote in 1853, entitled *The
Captive in Patagonia*.

As the *Allyne* anchored in a deserted cove on the wild South
American coast of Patagonia, Bourne set off in a small boat with
three other crewmen to shoot some sea birds. Nearing the shore
they spied a group of natives emerging from the shelter of the
rocks. They indicated that they wanted to trade and gestured to the
sailors to come closer. Wary as to whether this would be a good
idea, the men stayed off shore and tried to communicate with the
natives. But the tide was going out and the boat went aground.
Because the natives appeared friendly, the sailors waded ashore
and walked up the beach. The natives said that there were plenty
of eggs and beef at their village and they agreed to take the sailors
there. After considerable walking that seemed to lead nowhere,
Bourne became suspicious. He told his mates that they should
retreat back to the safety of the shore. But the natives blocked their
escape. They grabbed the men and disarmed them.

Bourne tried to convince the native chief that trading the
sailors for rum and tobacco would be a better alternative than just
killing them. The chief agreed but required that Bourne remain as
a hostage until the ransom was delivered. In the recounting of his
ordeal, Bourne admitted that he feared that he would never see his
friends again. "A sense of desolation came over me, at the thought
of being left alone in the power of these savages, of whose treachery and cunning I had already had such ample experience, and of
whose cruelty I had heard so much." He was taken to a hill above
the ship's anchorage to await the delivery of the ransom. Two small
boats from the *Allyne* approached the beach where the natives bade
them place the rum and tobacco on the sand. But when that was
done, the natives refused to release Bourne. His shipmates were
forced to return to their ship without him.

For several months Bourne was moved around the interior of
Patagonia. It was cold in the remote region. He was not dressed for

Benjamin F. Bourne. (Cape Cod Community College)

the weather and suffered greatly. What passed for food barely kept him alive. He began to despair for his life.

At some point, the natives discovered Bourne's pocket watch, which he had concealed in his vest. They demanded to know what it was. Bourne tried to explain its use but the natives were only fascinated with the instrument's steady ticking. The chief took the watch and placed it in his hut as a trophy. But within a day after appropriating this treasure the chief returned to Bourne. Why had the prize stopped its ticking? The chief wanted to know. Bourne was quick to recognize that with his timepiece, he had an instrument that might improve his circumstances of survival. With great ceremony, Bourne chanted some words and without letting the natives see what he was doing, he rewound the watch. The ticking started again.

Thinking that Bourne had some kind of a magic power, the chief allowed him to keep the watch on his person to guarantee its ticking. That sound, said Bourne, "struck awe over the tribe like the rod of an enchanter ... Forty times a day it had to be listened to." The natives were mesmerized by the device and "would stand in every attitude of silent amazement, their eyes dilated, their countenances lighted up in every feature with delighted wonder."

After almost two months, Bourne and his captors came to an island near the Santa Cruz River. There was a small European settlement there and the natives decided to use the same ransom ruse with Bourne as the bait. Concealing themselves behind some rocks, the natives instructed their captive to build a fire to draw the settlement's attention. He was to tell them that he was a shipwreck survivor in need of assistance. Several muscular natives crouched near him with knives drawn to prevent his escape.

As a boat approached from the settlement, Bourne waved his arms and tried to get the rowers to come closer. The sailors in the boat, not sure of what was happening and sensing danger, hesitated, laying on their oars about 50 yards off shore. For Bourne, it was now or never. He broke toward the water. As he did, several natives sprang up to intercept him. Knowing that his one chance of escape lay in somehow distracting his pursuers, Bourne grabbed the watch out of his pocket and held it in plain view. He then threw it as far away from him as he could and dove into the water. The natives scrambled for the watch and let him go. "My head was a great part of the time under water, my eyes blinded with the surf," he later recalled. As he neared the boat, hands reached out and pulled him in. "The shouts and screams of the Indians, which had followed me into the water, and rung hideously in my ears while struggling for life in the surf, were kept up till distance made them inaudible." The loss of his timepiece was a small price to pay for his freedom and Bourne wasted no time lamenting its loss. "Whether they found the watch, whose mysterious tick at once awed and delighted them and restored it to its place of state in the chief's lodge, or whether it still lies rusting in the sands by the sea-shore, is a problem unsolved."

Bourne stayed on the island recovering his strength and spirits for about a month. He left the small settlement aboard the whaler *Hudson* out of Mystic, Connecticut. Later, he transferred to the schooner *Hopewell*, which was bound for San Francisco. He reached there on February 19, 1850, one year and seven days from the date of his original departure from New Bedford. Bourne's two brothers had already established a gold mine about 70 miles east of San Francisco. After a week of looking for them, he found the claim. His brothers were amazed at his story. They had long ago accepted the fact that he was dead.

The Incredible Saga of the *Wild Wave*

On February 9, 1858, Captain Josiah Knowles departed San Francisco for New York in the 1,500-ton clipper ship *Wild Wave*. Save for the loss of a crewman over the side in the first week of the voyage, the trip south toward the Horn was uneventful. The ship was logging extended periods of 10 to 13-knot speeds and the 27-year old captain was confident that with continued good winds and weather, his ship would arrive in New York sometime in May. He was thinking of being able to spend a bit of time at home with his family on the Cape. Captain Knowles had no idea that circumstances were about to force him to embark on one of the great sea adventures of the century.

It was late in the evening on March 5, as the clipper moved south on her track in the vicinity of 24 degrees south latitude and 130 degrees east longitude, that the captain was awakened in his cabin by the shout of "Breakers under the lee!" by one of the ship's lookouts. Having carefully checked his charts and position prior to turning in, Captain Knowles was astonished that the *Wild Wave* was anywhere near land. Yet as he came up on deck, he could see a line of breakers dead ahead. Even as he gave the command to put the ship's wheel hard over, it was clear to him that there would be no escape for the *Wild Wave*. She slammed into a coral reef at great speed. The impact caused the ships masts to snap forward. With confusion on deck and pieces of copper bottom sheathing breaking loose and rigging stays flying around, Captain Knowles rallied his men to action. They cut away the masts to steady the vessel against a good surf that surged across the slanting deck. Fortunately, the ship had wedged herself so solidly into the reef that there was no immediate danger that she might sink, but a large and visible hole in the hull made it immediately clear that the *Wild Wave* had reached her final resting place.

In the morning, Captain Knowles took stock of his situation. His 30-man crew and ten passengers were amazingly unharmed and the sea had subsided enough so that the ship's boats could be put over the side. The captain ordered several crewmembers to row into the nearby lagoon and survey the small atoll which lay before them. It proved to be Oeno Island, a small, uninhabited piece of ground, not much more than a sandbar covered with palm trees. For some reason, navigation charts had incorrectly placed the island about 20 miles to the west. Reliance on this faulty chart proved fatal to the *Wild Wave*.

Once it was determined that there was a source of fresh water on the island, Captain Knowles got his crew and passengers off in the boats and they settled ashore in tents made from salvaged sail canvas. A walk around the two-mile long spit revealed that there were enough birds, fish, and clams for survival. But, the real question in the minds of all of the survivors was whether anyone would ever look for them in this remote corner of the Pacific Ocean.

Oeno Island, despite its ability to sustain the castaways, proved to be what Captain Knowles described as "a dreary waste of sand." Tropical heat burned the survivors of the *Wild Wave* by day. At night, rats that apparently had reached the island from an earlier shipwreck swarmed over the salvaged supplies. The survivors had to be constantly on alert to avoid being bitten by the army of aggressive land crabs. After a week of burning signal fires and not seeing any passing ships, Captain Knowles suggested a bold plan to save his crew and passengers. He estimated that Pitcairn Island was about eighty miles to the south of Oeno. He proposed taking one of the ship's boats, with a few volunteers, and sail to that British possession to gain assistance. On March 13, Captain Knowles, his first mate, and five crewmen departed Oeno for the voyage to Pitcairn Island.

It took just two days to reach Pitcairn Island. It stood bold and inaccessible as the captain and his crew looked for a safe landfall. They were able to land their small boat on the rugged shore and pulled it beyond the surf. The island was strangely quiet. The reason was soon made clear as the men read notices posted on trees revealing that two years earlier the islanders had been evacuated by the British government to Norfolk Island. Pitcairn was silent and abandoned.

At least food was not a problem. Chickens and goats—even a few cattle—apparently left behind when the inhabitants had been removed, provided a solid diet of meat. There were also vegetables and fruit trees and abundant sources of fresh water. But, as Captain Knowles ruefully acknowledged, there was little reason for any ships to call at this remote place and he and his crew were left in a relatively comfortable but potentially permanent island prison. They expected that the survivors on Oeno might follow them to Pitcairn after a reasonable time of waiting. But any thoughts of returning to Oeno were lost when their boat was pounded to pieces in a heavy surf.

With this new development, and after waiting several weeks without any signs of a ship, Captain Knowles decided that their only hope of rescue was to build a boat and sail to Tahiti, some 1,500 miles away. But the men had few tools and no seasoned lumber. Any boat would have to be built from scratch and with whatever tools they could salvage from the abandoned island houses. The men set about their task, hacking and shaping tree trunks into planks with hand axes. Burning several houses gave them a supply of nails and they salvaged pieces of cloth and canvas found within the abandoned dwellings for sails.

It took almost two months for the boat to be finished. Named the *John Adams* after one of the first settlers of Pitcairn Island, she was about 30 feet in length and was schooner rigged. The mainmast came from the flagpole that had overlooked the abandoned settlement. With three of the crewmembers deciding to stay on Pitcairn, the others put to sea on July 23rd. They had been marooned on Pitcairn almost three months. Contrary winds caused Captain Knowles to alter his course away from Tahiti and toward the Marquesas. Navigating by the stars, the captain estimated that they were making about 100 miles a day. A little more than a week later they sighted land. Being careful to avoid inhabited islands out of fear of cannibals, the little vessel skirted several small islands until arriving at Nukahiva in the Marquesas.

Captain Knowles was already preparing the men for the possibility that they would have to sail another 2,500 miles north to the Sandwich Islands if there was no help there. But at last the fates were kind to the survivors of the *Wild Wave*. As they rounded the point that shielded the lagoon at Nukahiva, they were astonished to find the American warship, *USS Vandalia*, at anchor there. She had arrived just one day before and was already making ready to leave for Tahiti. The *Vandalia* was the first ship that the survivors had seen in the almost six months since they had departed from San Francisco.

The crew of the *Vandalia* made the survivors welcome and marveled at their story. The warship headed to Tahiti where Captain Knowles recovered his strength and eventually was able to get back to San Francisco aboard a French ship. From there he made the trip back to the east coast aboard the steamer *Golden Gate,* arriving in New York in late October. Even though his family had been alerted about his rescue, when Captain Knowles walked into his Brewster house on November 1st it was to his relatives as if someone had returned from the dead. And indeed, that might almost have described what Captain Knowles had done.

The *USS Vandalia* sailed from Tahiti to Oeno and picked up the *Wild Wave's* remaining survivors. Though the conditions had been harsh, incredibly, only one man had died in the interim. The three men who had chosen to stay behind on Pitcairn Island were also rescued by the *Vandalia*, completing the tale of voyage and rescue that had started on a dark night some six months earlier with the cry, "Breakers under the lee!"

Captain Knowles was carrying two things of importance aboard the *Wild Wave*. One was $18,000 in gold that he had been charged with transferring back to New York. The second was a personal item, the body of his brother Thomas who had died and had been buried in San Francisco in 1852. Captain Knowles had temporarily re-buried his brother's casket on Oeno after the wreck. When the *Vandalia* went to Oeno to pick up the castaways, Thomas Knowles' body was retrieved. Taken to San Francisco, it was eventually shipped back to Cape Cod. As for the gold, it too arrived safely back on the east coast in a container that, in all the six months of travail at sea, had never left the sight of Captain Josiah Knowles.

Swallowed by a Whale

In the long history of whaling, the ultimate struggle between man and creature often came down to "a dead whale, or a stove boat." The image that Melville weaves in the classic nineteenth century novel *Moby Dick* has the maniacal Ahab solidly fast to his nemesis whale as it sounds in its death knell, bringing the captain to his own final end in the fathomless deep. In some ways, Melville might have anticipated the 1860 story of Job Sherman, who was third mate aboard the Fairhaven whaler, *Mary Ann*.

Sherman narrowly escaped death in the maw of an angry sperm whale. In a newspaper account, his situation was described thusly: "Both legs were in his mouth ... Fortunately the whale soon came up so the man could breathe. In the meantime, he had extricated one of his legs. But the whale immediately went down again carrying Mr. Sherman down the second time. He was able to use his sheath knife against the whale's under jaw and it let go of him. He [Mr. Sherman] came up about a ship's length from a whaleboat. On examination, he found himself minus his pants, and with a hole in one leg large enough to receive an egg."

There are many examples of Cape Cod whalemen getting a good dunking in their quest for "greasy luck." Some lost their lives to angry whales. But in at least several cases, the intervention of fate saved the whaleman from death and, whether by pure luck or

Divine intervention, the sailor lived for another day. These lucky individuals were the "Jonahs" of Cape Cod.

Caleb Osborn Hamblin of Falmouth was the second mate aboard the whaler *Congress* when, in 1858, his whaleboat was attacked by a sperm whale. When the boat was upended, Hamblin found himself suddenly perched astride the whale's lower jaw with a leg in the corner of its mouth. Fortunately, the creature did not clamp down hard on him. When the whale sounded, Hamblin had the presence of mind to grab on to a line that was still fast to the overturned boat. About twenty feet down, he was literally torn out of the whale's mouth and he rose back to the surface. Pulled to safety by other sailors, Hamblin eventually threw the fatal harpoon that dispatched the whale.

In 1863, Peleg Nye was a crewmember aboard the Provincetown whaler *C.W. Lewis*. Near the Cape Verde Islands, a sperm whale was spotted and the boats were lowered to give chase. Upon reaching the whale, Nye followed the boatsteerer's harpoon thrust with a bomb lance. The combination of the two instruments should have killed the creature, but instead the whale slapped its tail, smashing off the boat's bow. All of the men went into the water. Nye, because he was up forward, fell into the whale's open mouth and he was pinned, vice-like, in the jaw by his legs. In one way he had been fortunate. The teeth of the whale did not crush his legs, but as he struggled to free himself, the creature began a descent toward the bottom.

Nye later recalled that he hammered ineffectually on the whale's head with his fists, but then blacked out. He could see the sunlight receding above. A second whaleboat circled the spot where the whale had sounded and picked up some of the crew. Amazingly, Nye's unconscious body came up right next to the boat and he was pulled to safety. The whale had momentarily released him, opening its jaw in its death throes. After a lengthy period, Nye recovered. He did not let the incident sour him on the seagoing life and he stayed active in whaling for over 50 years. The Sandwich-born sailor became a captain in his own right and lived until his "final voyage over the bar" in Hyannis in July of 1896.

A third Cape Codder who had a near death experience with a whale was Franklin Atkins of Provincetown. Like Nye and

Hamblin, Atkins was also tossed into the water by a sperm whale. When his small whaleboat was overturned by the whale's flukes, Atkins landed in the creature's open mouth. The whale's teeth scarred his legs and broke some of his bones. But Atkins was spit out by the whale before it dove below and he was picked up by another boat, more dead than alive. Long after he recovered, he carried a frightful scar on his back and side from the effects of the whale's teeth. Had the whale clamped down hard, Atkins would have been crushed. In his declining years, he was a fixture along the Provincetown waterfront and he was never shy about his adventure. As he put it, "Me and Jonah were the only two persons that had been into a whale's mouth and come out alive."

Confederate Raiders and Cape Cod Ships
When the Civil War began in the spring of 1861, American maritime fortunes were at their height. Ship tonnage exceeded that of every country in the world and the major ocean routes were dominated by U.S. companies. By 1865, when the conflict ended, these interests had been decimated to the point where they never recovered. The proud tradition of a seafaring nation and the fortunes of people who were connected with the shipping industry went into steady decline.

Perhaps no group suffered more than the shipping interests of Massachusetts and by association, Cape Codders. The captains of ships from this area—many of whom were part owners of the vessels they operated—were especially hurt.

In April of 1861, at the outset of the conflict, the Confederate government authorized Letters of Marque for privateers, setting aside a 20% bounty on captured Yankee ships. Within a month, the rebel government had received over 3,000 applications. With virtually no navy of its own, and with 90% of American shipping owned by northern interests, the resort to privateering was a logical step for the Confederacy. And without an effective blockade of southern ports by the federal navy, privateers were free to prey on unarmed merchantmen and whalers from Galveston, Texas to Norfolk, Virginia.

In early June, the privateer *Calhoun* seized three Provincetown whalers in the Caribbean, the *John Adams*, the *Mermaid*, and the

Panama. The prizes were taken to New Orleans. In that same month, Captain Joshua Eldridge of Barnstable had his bark *Nueces* seized by rebels at Galveston, Texas. The Confederate privateers *Jeff Davis* and *Winslow* were active in the waters between Nassau and Cape Hatteras. In July of 1861, the *Winslow* captured the 198-ton schooner *Herbert Manton* and her cargo of sugar. Her captain, Simeon Backus of Marstons Mills and his crew were taken prisoner and brought to New Bern, North Carolina where they were held for almost a month before being released and sent north without their ship. A month later, the rebel steamer *Sumter* captured the schooner *Abby Bradford* commanded by Captain Ezra Freeman of Sandwich off Porto Cabello.

As the Union blockade became more effective, the Confederates contracted to have vessels constructed in Great Britain, and the tactics turned to destruction rather than capture. The *Sumter, Alabama, Florida, Tallahassee,* and *Shenandoah* were perhaps the most famous of these commerce raiders, but there were a number of others as well. Slipping out of southern ports, these ships destroyed hundreds of Union ships on the high seas. Insurance rates skyrocketed and many northern ship owners moved their ships to neutral registry.

The 220-foot, heavily gunned *Alabama* was the most feared of the Confederate raiders. Under the command of the South's most famous captain, Raphael Semmes, the raider cut a swath through Union shipping that continued until her destruction by the *U.S.S. Kearsarge* in 1864. In 1862, the *Alabama* captured and sank a number of whaling ships, including four from Cape Cod and the Islands. The *Ocmulgee* from Edgartown was destroyed in September and several weeks later, the *Ocean* from Sandwich went to the bottom. The *Weather Guage* and the *Courser*, both from Provincetown, were burned near the Azores in the same month. Semmes used the *Courser* as a practice target for his gunners.

On October 15th, the *Alabama* took the 370-ton *Lamplighter*, commanded by Captain Orrin V. Harding of Chatham. Bound for Gibraltar with a load of tobacco, the bark was boarded in mid-Atlantic. Captain Harding was received cordially by Captain Semmes aboard the rebel steamer. But when he tried to dissuade Semmes from seizing his ship, the Confederate captain said, "he hoped to serve him a damned site worse." The pirates boarded the *Lamplighter*, ripped open the mattresses, broke up the furniture, and then set the vessel afire. Captain Harding and his crew were kept in irons for two weeks until they were transferred to the bark *Baron de Castine*. The survivors arrived in Boston on November 2, 1862.

The *T.B. Wales*, commanded by Captain Edgar Lincoln of Brewster, was the next victim of the *Alabama*. The *Wales* was from Calcutta, bound for Boston in November when she was taken in mid-Atlantic. The Confederate ship had run up a flag indicating that she was the U.S. Sloop of War *Tuscarora*. Taken in by the ruse, Captain Lincoln was forced to hand over his ship to the rebels. The ship and her cargo, together valued at over $250,000, were burned.

Captain Francis Hinckley of Barnstable lost his ship, the *Star of Peace*, to the Confederate raider *Florida* in 1863. Sailing to Boston from the port of Liverpool, the *Star of Peace* carried a cargo worth over a half million dollars. On March 6th, a steamer flying the American flag came up on Captain Hinckley's ship. As it grew closer, it hauled down the Stars and Stripes and ran up the Confederate flag. A shot was fired across the bow of the *Star of Peace* and she was forced to heave to. As Captain Hinckley watched from the deck of the *Florida*, his 1,000-ton ship was set afire and sent to the bottom. Before she sank beneath the waves, the fire set off a tremendous explosion. The rebel captain, John Maffitt, noted in his log that, "A most beautiful panorama was never witnessed on the ocean."

The clipper ship *Southern Cross*, commanded by Benjamin P. Howes of Dennis, also fell victim to the *Florida* later that spring off the coast of Brazil. With only a half hour to take whatever he could carry, he and his wife Lucy, along with the rest of the crew, were brought by long boat to the raider. When asked what the rebel captain was going to do with his ship, the reply was, "Burn her, of course." And that is what happened. Howes and his wife were eventually transferred to a French ship, which took them to a Brazilian port. They arrived back on Cape Cod in September.

Another Brewster sea captain who narrowly escaped capture by a southern raider was James Dillingham Jr. In 1863, while commanding the clipper ship *Snow Squall*, and sailing off the coast of southern Africa, Dillingham saw a bark closing on his stern. She was flying the American flag. As the two ships closed, the stranger revealed herself to be the Confederate raider *Tuscaloosa*. Her captain signaled Dillingham that he intended to board the *Snow Squall*. But the Cape skipper knew he had a good ship under him and decided to make a run for it. "Requesting my wife to return to the cabin, I ordered the helm hove up and all possible sail made," he wrote in a later newspaper account. After heaving some of the cargo overboard to lighten his ship, the clipper began to inch out of the range of the slower *Tuscaloosa's* guns. "At about 6 o'clock, the chase swung broadside to and fired a shot at us, but without effect, and then continued the chase. Soon after this, finding we were distancing him, we desisted from lightening the ship, all hands uniting in thanks to God for his gracious deliverance."

Ironically, Captain Dillingham later encountered another Confederate raider under very different circumstances. About a year later, while still in command of the *Snow Squall*, Captain Dillingham had the misfortune to run aground at Tierra del Fuego near the tip of South America. The ship began to leak and the only option was to bring her to Port Stanley in the Falkland Islands. Once there, and after several months of repair efforts, it was ascertained that the ship could not economically be salvaged. Finishing up the *Snow Squall's* business and selling what he could from the hulk, Captain Dillingham got himself to Rio de Janeiro where he boarded a Baltimore-bound ship, the *Mondamin*. A few days out, the *Mondamin* was captured by the *C.S.S. Florida*. It had taken two rebel commanders and two different raiders, but James Dillingham was finally a Confederate prisoner! It was several months before he was able to get home to Boston where he took a break from seafaring, admitting to friends that "he was all used up."

Ten years after the war, the American war claims against Great Britain for building ships for the Confederacy were settled. Among the premiums awarded by the Court of Commissioners were: to Captain Francis Hinckley, $1,450 for loss of personal possessions by the destruction of the ship *Star of Peace*; to Abraham Phinney, $633 for loss of personal effects in the destruction of the ship *Mondamin*; to Abraham Phinney, $852.50 for loss of same in the destruction of the brig *Clarence*; to Silas Young, $866.66 for losses sustained in the destruction of the schooner *Courser* (plus $1,200 for lost wages); and to Henry Cook, $200 for the loss of his chronometer by the destruction of the schooner *Weather Guage*. Despite an elaborate and detailed inventory of personal items he claimed had been seized by the *Florida*, Captain James Dillingham received nothing. His case was dismissed by the claims court.

"A Confusion of Angry Waters"

The Life Saving Service was established in the late 19th century to assist ships in distress along the Atlantic shore. Literally hundreds of wrecks took place before steam replaced sail and there were many cases where Cape Codders risked their lives to bring shipwrecked sailors to safety. Certainly, one example that demonstrates the willingness to undertake the dangerous task of pulling sailors off a stranded hulk is the rescue of the crew of the schooner *Grecian* in December of 1885.

The ill-fated schooner had left Calais, Maine with a load of coal and was bound for New York City. On the night of December 5th she was in trouble off Chatham about three miles south of the Chatham Life Saving Station. The weather was nasty and a gale blew up during the night with sleet and rain. Around two o'clock in the morning, the ship's anchors began to drag. Attempting to get under way and run before the storm, the *Grecian* lost her foremast and jib in the howling wind and became unmanageable. In short order she was stranded on a sand bar. The vessel lay about 400 yards off shore and began to fill with water as a heavy sea broke over her. The five crewmen fired shotguns to attract attention and clung to the deckhouse in the freezing cold.

The shots caught the attention of a group of wreckers on the shore. George Bloomer and Benjamin Patterson put together two crews and launched boats into the breakers to effect a rescue. Visibility was near zero as the two boats pulled for the wreck. Years later, Cape author Joseph Crosby Lincoln, in researching material for his novel *Rugged Water*, interviewed some of the individuals that had been involved in the rescue effort and he wrote perhaps one of the most vivid and realistic summaries of just how difficult the conditions must have been. In his story, he clearly had the *Grecian's* rescue in mind, as the circumstances of the wreck were similar. One of Lincoln's characters was an Ed Bloomer. "After a half hour of weary battling with the screaming gale, they dropped the sail and took up the oars. The exercise was welcome, for the cold was piercing beyond belief. The flying spray froze almost as soon as it struck. The boat, inside and out, was soon coated with ice. The men's shoulders, their sou'westers, their eyebrows and eyelashes and mustaches were hung with icicles. Their mittens were armored gauntlets hooked about the oar handles. Calvin, swinging at the steering oar at the stern, was a glistening statue. The seas were so high that, in the hollows between them, the force of the wind noticeably abated and it was not until they climbed to the next crest that it struck them with the whole of its cruel force."

As the two boats neared the stranded *Grecian*, they had to maneuver through what was described in a later report summary as "a confusion of angry waters." Once in the lee of the wreck, the rescuers tied along side and pulled the five men off the deckhouse to safety. The row back toward shore had its own dangers, especially as the rescuers had to precisely time the breakers to carry them to the beach. They were all on dry land as the sun came up on the morning of December 6th.

While Bloomer and his two crews were battling the waves, the crew from the Chatham Life Saving Station, now alerted to the *Grecian's* plight, put its own surfboat into the water. But by the time they arrived at the stricken vessel, the castaways had already been

Launching into the breakers. (Jim Coogan collection)

removed. Even so, their futile effort was no less brave. The survivors were eventually taken to the Lifesaving Station where they were warmed up and given dry clothes. A day later, they were on their way back to their homes in Maine.

For their valiant efforts, the participants in the *Grecian* rescue were awarded the silver lifesaving medal. These men included George Bloomer, Benjamin Patterson, Andrew Bearse, Zenas Hawes, Otis Eldredge, Zenas Gould, Francisco Bloomer, Willis Bearse, and Wilber Patterson.

"Surfman Higgins has just burned his signal!"

That was the cry from the observation deck at the Pamet River Life Saving Station in Truro on a December night a little more than a century ago. It was the winter of 1893 when the Scottish ship *Jason* miscalculated her final approach into Boston Harbor and ran aground near the Truro station.

Surfman Higgins had been watching the laboring ship for several hours as she tried to escape the northeast wind that was steadily driving her toward the shore. The keepers at the Nauset Life Saving Station and at Cahoon's Hollow had also been following the ship's progress during the day and had updated each other by telephone. With a voyage originating in Calcutta, India—half a world away—the *Jason* was within just a few hours of Boston when, in a driving sleet and heavy fog, the 1,500-ton full rigged ship struck several hundred yards off shore near Ballston Beach. When that happened, Surfman Higgins fired his flare. The waves smashed the ship's boats against the steel hull. The crew, left with no means of getting off the stranded ship, climbed into the mizzen shrouds. But the *Jason* couldn't take the relentless pounding of the surf and quickly broke in half. In the ship's death throes, her slatting sails sounded like distant thunder and the rigging blocks and chains gave off sparks as they were flung about by the wind.

Unable to launch a surfboat in the fierce storm, rescuers tried to shoot a line across the vessel but the half-frozen survivors couldn't get to it. When the main and mizzenmasts fell, the crewmen were swept to their deaths in the frigid sea. All of the 24-man crew except for one man was lost. Seaman Samuel Evans rode a bale of jute through the surf where he was picked up, half dead from exposure. He was taken to the Life Saving Station where, with warm blankets and the ministering of the Pamet River station crew, he survived.

The next day, the outer beach was strewn with the ship's wreckage. Bits and pieces of the tragedy littered the sand for miles. The debris field from the *Jason* covered a wide swath along the Cape's backside. Human remains were scattered among the wreckage and twenty bodies were eventually recovered. Later they were buried in a common grave in Wellfleet. Some were never identified. Four were never found. The battered hulk of the *Jason* lay on its side in two separate pieces, her erect foremast still holding shredded sails at a crazy angle. Within weeks, all evidence of the vessel was erased by the swirling seas. She had come so far, only to become another grim statistic in the Cape's long history of maritime disasters.

As for the one survivor, seaman Evans, he seemed reconciled that the fates weren't ready to take him on that cold December night, and he eventually went back to sea again. Evans was a man who believed that what is written couldn't be altered. Some years later, again on the wide ocean, fate intervened a second time and he lost his life in another ship.

Old Harbor Life Saving Station. (Jack Sheedy photo)

Chapter 6

Tales True, Upon the Ocean Blue

Over the centuries, tales have been told of Cape Codders upon the ocean blue. Some of these salty tales tell of the human nature of the participants involved. Some tell of their decisions and the sometimes unfortunate consequences. And some tell of their exploits, unusual but true.

"That Settles it!"
Sea voyages have always involved the keeping of a daily logbook of the ship's activities for each twenty-four hour period. Normally log entries were made by the captain or the first mate. Sometimes they shared the duty. Winds, weather, position, and distance traveled were regular entries in the ship's log. Occasional recording of specific or unusual events can also be found, such as vessels spoken, whales taken, or perhaps issues with the crew. But in at least one instance, the logbook was used as an instrument to effect a change in behavior—with an unusual result.

Captain Allen Hallett, a blue water skipper from Hyannis, was on a voyage from New York to the West Indies. Just a few days out, the ship ran into a tremendous gale which put a heavy strain on the vessel. To keep the ship afloat, the crew had to maintain stations for almost two days.

The first mate was having problems with an infected tooth. The constant pitch and roll of the ship, coupled with his painful affliction, had the man in agony. To alleviate his discomfort, he slipped below and began to nip on a bottle of spirits. In short order he was unfit for duty. Captain Hallett was aware of what the mate was doing and decided to discipline him by making an entry into the logbook. After each regular notation, the captain added the embarrassing words, "The mate is drunk," or "The mate is still drunk." When the unfortunate mate recovered enough to resume his duties, he read the logbook and reacted hotly. "Captain, I did not think you would do such a dirty trick as to put in the log that I was drunk." Captain Hallett replied, "Well, you was drunk, weren't you?" The usually reliable mate admitted that this had indeed been the case. "Well, that settles it!" said the captain and the entries stayed a part of the ship's record.

Later, on the return leg of the voyage, Captain Hallett happened to take a look at the logbook which the first mate had been keeping. He found an entry that read, "The Captain is sober." A few pages later he noticed another one that read, "The Captain is still sober." Confronting his mate, Captain Hallett indignantly asked what was the meaning of the entries. "Well," said the mate, "You was sober, weren't you?" The captain admitted that indeed this was the case. "That settles it, then!" said the mate and the entries stayed a part of the ship's record.

While some might have seen this as an act of insubordination by the mate, Captain Hallett didn't view it that way. When the ship arrived in New York, he recommended the mate for a command of his own. "With brass like that," reasoned the skipper, "He had all of the qualities to be a natural."

"Mad Jack" and the Missionaries
There are few characters in Cape Cod history that come close to approaching the larger than life persona of Captain John "Mad Jack" Percival of West Barnstable. His exploits from the War of 1812 through his taking the USS Constitution around the world in 1844 near the end of a long naval career have been told and re-told. He was, as they say, a "colorful" personality. As one official put it, one couldn't be certain as to whether Percival was a naval officer or a pirate. But perhaps the one story that cemented his reputation as a maverick was his tussle with the missionaries in the Sandwich Islands, now Hawaii.

In 1825, while in command of the schooner USS Dolphin, Percival had been dispatched by the government to the Pacific in search of the mutineers from the Nantucket whaler Globe. After successfully finding out what had happened during that infamous mutiny and rescuing two survivors of the tragedy, Percival sailed to the Sandwich Islands. His mission was to show the flag and make sure that American ships were receiving the same privileges as other foreign vessels in the island kingdom. When the *Dolphin* arrived in Oahu in January of 1826 it was the first American Navy vessel to visit Hawaii.

Upon arrival, Percival found that American missionaries had inserted themselves into the island's politics. In their zeal to convert the natives to Christianity, the missionaries were advising the ruling chiefs on matters from trade policy to morality. And they had convinced the locals that they were representing the United States government. Percival quickly made it clear that as the ranking military officer present, he was the only representative of the government in the islands. This put him in direct conflict with Hiram Bingham, who was the head missionary in Hawaii. Bingham's reputation was such that he was referred to in private as the "Pope" of the islands. The two men clashed from the beginning and Percival's brusque manner didn't smooth things over. One contemporary described "Mad Jack" as "extremely profane, very abusive in his language, and of a most ungovernable temper." None of these attributes Captain Percival would have denied.

Just three months before the arrival of the *Dolphin*, the missionary group had convinced the chiefs to stop allowing the island girls to swim out to visit the Western ships that were anchoring off the port. As in many of the Pacific islands, this welcome had been eagerly anticipated by sailors who were looking for some female companionship. When they learned that the practice had been made taboo, they were on the verge of rioting. Percival had not wanted to be drawn into that particular controversy, but when he was informed that just a few months before his arrival a British ship, the *HMS Blonde*, had been allowed to have girls aboard, he felt that "visiting privileges" were not being awarded fairly.

Some accounts have indicated that Percival threatened to blow up the town if the restriction on women wasn't lifted. Percival later admitted to have used some rough language and perhaps a veiled threat or two, but blowing up the town was not what he had said. To him it was a misunderstanding. But shortly after what was probably a bluff, a number of sailors, including some from the

Dolphin, went ashore on a Sunday and threatened to kill the missionaries unless the ban on the girls was relaxed. A general riot ensued and damage was done to the mission property.

Captain Percival took immediate action to stop the marauding sailors and sent some of the ringleaders back to his own ship to be flogged. But later, when he sat down with the island chiefs—with the missionary representatives not present—he counseled the native leaders that the ban on women was both inflammatory and impossible to enforce. To the shock of the missionaries, who saw the action as promoting prostitution, Percival convinced the chiefs to lift the ban. The next day, to the cheers of all of the sailors in the harbor, the women were back on the anchored ships. There were no more riots for the remainder of the time the *Dolphin* stayed in Hawaii.

The matter, however, didn't end with Percival's departure from the islands in May of 1826. A vicious letter writing campaign was initiated by the missionary group and many of their accounts of Percival's actions began to show up in American newspapers. The powerful religious lobby went after Percival's conduct and his failure to support their efforts to Christianize the natives. By the time Percival arrived home the issue had reached a furor and the captain found himself and some of his officers accused of promoting lawlessness and sin in the islands. He requested a naval court of inquiry to clear his name and after two years of deliberation, both he and his officers were exonerated of any wrongdoing. The supporters of the missionaries were furious. But in reading the decision, it was clear that the Navy department believed that Percival could have been far more judicious in both his actions and his words in handling the matter. His vindication was as much a censure as it was a vote of support. While he did get command of another ship in 1830 and was promoted to Commander a year later, the matter continued to dog his reputation for years afterward.

The charge that Percival encouraged prostitution in Hawaii probably doesn't bear up under examination. That he detested the puritanical missionary cabal—especially Hiram Bingham—is quite clear. He felt that they had overstepped their mandate and in their zealotry had gotten involved in matters reserved for the American government. As to the shipboard visits by island girls, Percival, like all military commanders, probably understood that some controlled licentiousness aboard ship was far preferable to uncontrolled sin and mayhem on shore. In that, at least, "Mad Jack" Percival was a most practical man.

Hannah Rebecca's Well Traveled Bible

Hannah Rebecca Crowell Burgess of Sandwich is perhaps the most well known seafaring woman from Cape Cod. Married to Captain William Burgess, she made a voyage out to the Far East in 1853 aboard his clipper ship *Whirlwind*. During that voyage she learned celestial navigation to accurately compute the ship's position. On a subsequent voyage in 1856, aboard the clipper *Challenger*, Captain Burgess was taken ill about 600 miles off the South American coast. Hannah Rebecca used her navigation skills to successfully bring the ship into Valparaiso, Chile. Sadly, Captain Burgess did not recover from his sickness and Hannah was left to make arrangements to have her husband's remains shipped back to Sandwich.

Throughout all of her difficulties, Mrs. Burgess' steward, David Graves, stood by her, attending to her needs and serving as a source of strength for the young widow. When she returned home, Hannah made a gift of her Bible to her faithful friend. Graves later shipped out on the clipper *Ringleader*, commanded by Captain Otis White of Yarmouth. In a May 1863 typhoon, the *Ringleader*, bound from Hong Kong to San Francisco with a cargo of Chinese coolies, was blown ashore on the island of Formosa (Taiwan). The ship was a total loss. Graves, as did most of the crew, survived the wreck but escaped with just the clothes on his back.

Several days after the wreck, an American named Dennison visited the *Ringleader's* remains and, picking through what had been left by the salvagers, he spied a Bible. Inside he noted the inscription, "Presented to David Graves by Mrs. Rebecca H. Burgess, Boston, February 10, 1857." Dennison sent the Bible to a friend in Hong Kong who arranged to have it delivered to attorney Richard Henry Dana in Boston. Dana, who had carved his own history aboard sailing ships before beginning his law practice, placed an advertisement in a Boston newspaper asking if anyone might be able to identify the book's original owner. Less than a week later, Hannah Burgess read the notice and recognized her gift to her former steward. She contacted Dana and the Bible was returned to her. Today it is part of the Hannah Burgess collection at the Sandwich Glass Museum in Sandwich.

Cape Cod's Japanese Connection

New England's connection to the China trade started in the late 18th century with the arrival at Canton in 1784 of the ship *Empress of China*. Cape Cod skippers were soon heavily engaged in the shipping of tea, silk, and porcelain back to American ports. But the island of Japan remained closed to the outside world and only a handful of westerners were able to penetrate its mystery.

Captain Peter Childs of North Falmouth was one of the first American whaling masters to enter a Japanese port. In 1847, when they arrived there, his wife Cordelia was a source of fascination to the Japanese. She was probably the first white woman to set foot in the kingdom. Another person with Cape Cod roots was instrumental a few years later in forcing Japan to open some of her ports to western trade. U.S. Navy Commodore Matthew Perry was a descendant of Edward Perry, who arrived in Sandwich in 1640 and who eventually married Mary Freeman, the daughter of one of Sandwich's founding fathers. In 1861, another Cape Codder, John Wilson of Barnstable, moved to Yeddo (Tokyo) to work as a photographer. There is evidence that while there, Wilson influenced Renjo Shimooka, one of Japan's most famous pioneer photographers. But perhaps the most interesting story of Cape Cod's connection to Japan is that of a young Japanese man who came to America as a stowaway and became the adopted son of a Cape Cod sea captain.

When Salem Captain William Savory was preparing to leave the northern Japanese port of Hakodate in late 1864, he discovered that one of his passengers was aboard without the permission of Japanese authorities. It had been just a little over a decade since Perry's historic visit and Japan was still very much a strange and little known world for Americans. For their part, the Japanese were wary of letting their people leave the island country. There were severe penalties for those who attempted to do so and few had tried.

Twenty-one year old Shimeta Neesima, the son of a lower level Samurai government worker, was hidden below decks by the ship's crew until the port inspectors departed the ship. Only when well out to sea did Captain Savory call for the young man to emerge from his hiding place. Unable to master the man's Japanese name, the captain settled on "Joe" as an easier substitute. During the voyage from Japan to Shanghai, China, "Joe" Neesima told the captain of his interest in Christianity and his dreams of being one of the first from his country to visit the United States. Once in the Chinese port, the castaway was introduced to Captain Horace Taylor of Chatham, who was in command of the medium clipper *Wild Rover*. Captain Taylor agreed to take "Joe" Neesima aboard as a cabin boy and servant.

During the voyage back to Boston, Neesima practiced his English and worked on his navigation. When the *Wild Rover* arrived at its homeport, Captain Taylor brought him to the office of Captain Alpheus Hardy, the owner of the ship. Hardy, also from Chatham, was intrigued by the young Japanese man and amazed by his story. As a member of the American Board of Commissioners for Foreign Missions, Hardy was particularly interested in Neesima's desire to return to Japan as a Christian missionary. Hardy made arrangements for Neesima to live at his Boston home for a period of time and through his connections as a trustee of Phillips Andover Academy and Amherst College, he secured a place for Neesima's schooling. With the financial support of his American "father," Neesima finished Phillips Academy and went on to graduate from Amherst College in 1870. He was the first of his countrymen to graduate from an American college. While at Andover Theological School, Neesima was baptized as a Christian and formally took the name "Joseph," after the Biblical figure. He also honored his mentor, Alpheus Hardy, using the family name as his middle name. Henceforth he was known as Joseph Hardy Neesima.

It was Neesima's intent to return to his country as a Christian missionary. As much as the religious philosophy appealed to the young Japanese man, it was probably just as much the fact that in that time, Christianity represented Western power. As a nationalist, Neesima wanted that power for Japan and he believed that Western style progress would follow the conversion of his country. While at Andover Theological School, young Neesima had the opportunity to serve as an interpreter for a Japanese delegation that had come to visit Massachusetts to study the education system. His assistance to the Imperial government guaranteed that he could safely go home without penalty. After a year of raising funds for his venture, he returned to Japan in 1874. Laws against the preaching of Christianity had been repealed the previous year and Neesima was able to establish a Christian school in Kyoto, calling it "Doshisha," which translates to mean "One Purpose." A number of young Samurai enrolled in the school and were converted to Christianity, and later these individuals became influential in the government. By the early 1880's, enrollment had reached almost 1,000 students.

In 1884, Neesima traveled to Europe and then to the United States where he was again reunited with his Chatham family. It was the last time Captain Hardy would see his adopted son. The Captain passed away in 1887. Three years later his protégé, Joseph Hardy Neesima, died near his beloved school in Japan. A year before his death, Neesima was awarded an honorary Doctor of Divinity degree by Amherst College, his alma mater.

When the Wrong Flag Cost a Ship

Sometimes it takes just a little mistake to forever alter a career. This was the case with a Cape skipper who made the mistake of flying the wrong flag.

It was April of 1865 when Captain John Eldridge of Barnstable sailed his whaler *Harvest* into the small harbor at Pohnpei in the Pacific Caroline Islands. Captain Eldridge was eager to get his vessel anchored and get ashore for a good night's rest. He noted that three other Yankee whalers were already in the harbor. As a sign of friendship, Eldridge ordered the American flag run up on the mast rather than the Hawaiian flag—the country that his vessel was actually registered with. It seemed a small gesture at the time, but it would cost Captain Eldridge his ship and affect the rest of his life.

Not long after *Harvest* had dropped anchor, a three-masted steam powered ship made its way into the tight anchorage. This new arrival flew the Confederate flag. It was the southern commerce raider *Shenandoah*. Before there could be any resistance, the rebel warship launched a raiding party and captured the surprised and unprepared whalers. Stating his intention to burn the Yankee vessels, Captain James Waddell sent an officer to Eldridge to tell him to get his personal belongings ashore. After inviting the officer on board,

Captain Eldridge explained that his vessel wasn't an American ship, but that she was really Hawaiian. He showed that *Harvest* was actually owned by Dowsett Brothers of Honolulu. The ship, he claimed, was not a proper prize of war because the independent Kingdom of Hawaii was not a belligerent with the Confederacy.

An officer who recorded the scene noted that Captain Waddell was not fooled by Captain Eldridge's ruse. "You came in flying the stars and stripes, didn't you?" asked the rebel commander. Eldridge admitted that indeed he had done this. "You and most of your crew are Americans, aren't you?" Eldridge admitted that it was so. Waddell replied, "Your fate will be the same as the others."

After Captain Waddell cleared his actions with the island king, who asked only that the four ships be scuttled away from the main channel to the harbor, his men set about burning the American whalers. Captain Eldridge looked on helplessly as *Harvest* went to the bottom. He and the rest of his men were put ashore on Pohnpei as the *Shenandoah* left for the Arctic where several months later the raider would sink many more Yankee ships.

Apparently so embarrassed by the loss of his whaler because of having made such a foolish mistake—the flying of the wrong flag—Captain Eldridge never returned to Cape Cod. He stayed on Pohnpei and eventually married a daughter of the king who gave him a good island so that he could make a living as a trader. But Captain Eldridge had no better luck ashore than he had as master of *Harvest*. A man who knew him in those days said that while an easygoing and quiet man, "he was too fond of the bottle, so he was always hard up." It wasn't long after that Captain Eldridge went to sea again as master of a small island schooner, *Malolo*. He held that position for less than a year. Later, he sailed around the Caroline Islands as a mate aboard a vessel owned by the notorious Bully Hayes. Records have Eldridge still living in the islands as late as 1883, remaining true to his vow to never return home. His final fate is unknown.

The Pickled Baby
In the nineteenth century many sea captains took their wives with them on long sea voyages. One of those captains was Seth Nickerson of Cotuit. Captain Nickerson, like many of his contemporaries, went to sea early as a cabin boy. By his twenties, he was

master of the 360-ton *Massachusetts*, a Pacific whaler. He had aboard with him his wife, Rosilla, and their infant daughter, Ella Caroline. At one point in the voyage, the ship made port in Callao, Peru where Captain Nickerson agreed to transport some treasure hunters to San Francisco. While en route to California, little Ella became ill and died. She was just a little over a year old.

Rosilla was adamant that her little girl would not be buried at sea, nor would she allow a burial in foreign soil. The decision was made to bring the child's remains home to Cape Cod. The ship's carpenter prepared a barrel and the body was immersed inside in a solution of rum cut with lime. The container was lashed to the stern rail of the ship and remained there until the ship reached Hawaii. There, a proper coffin was built and the baby's body was placed inside the zinc-lined container that was then sealed with solder. Thomas Chatfield, who was first mate on the *Massachusetts*, assisted in transferring the remains to the new casket. "Her little body was perfect in form," he recalled. "Only the skin slightly discolored, so it was brought home and buried in Cotuit."

Rosilla eventually had two more children after the death of Ella. Interestingly, the next child, a daughter born in 1852, was given the name Clara but was thereafter always referred to in the family as Ella Clara, no doubt in memory of the little life that had preceded her and had been lost so far from her native shores.

In much the same circumstance as the tragedy that befell Seth and Rosilla Nickerson, Captain Josiah Knowles and his wife, Mary, lost their eleven month old son, Thomas, in January of 1876 while aboard the clipper ship *Glory of the Seas*. The ship's carpenter was instructed to make a small box that could be filled with preservative. The child's remains were placed inside and carried to Liverpool, England, and eventually shipped to New Bedford where they were buried in Mary's family plot.

A version of this story was published in *Cape Cod Legends*, a 1935 Hyannis pamphlet published by the "Cape Cod Advancement Plan." But there was a twist. A woman named Lydia Russell Crocker gave birth to a child shortly after her husband had sailed on a long sea voyage. The baby died just a few months later. Determined that her husband should see his child, Lydia put the baby in a jar of alcohol and kept it until her husband returned home.

The story continued to say that for thirty years after, the pickled baby stayed in a closet and when Lydia died, it was buried with her.

"Chart George" Eldridge

In the nineteenth century, Vineyard Sound and Nantucket Sound were the second busiest shipping channels in the world after the English Channel. In those days of sail, and before the 1914 completion of the Cape Cod Canal, a trip around Cape Cod was a dangerous undertaking. As late as the 1840's there were few accurate charts to help mariners navigate the treacherous shoal waters off the coast. Chatham, at the Cape's elbow, was perhaps the most dangerous passage area and the shifting bars and channels there claimed many vessels. Recognizing this, local Captain George Eldridge began working on a study of local waters that would become a most important resource for sailors.

Captain Eldridge had been the master of a coasting vessel at the age of twenty, and he knew by experience the difficulties of transiting unfamiliar and shallow waters without accurate charts. His father, grandfather, and great-grandfather—all Chatham natives—had also been sea captains and several members of his extended family had been lost at sea after striking uncharted marine hazards.

George Eldridge did not have much formal schooling. He was a student of the sea by experience and an observer of how the wind and tides provided repeating patterns that could be predicted and used by sailors. Eldridge was particularly interested in the shift that took place in the Chatham inlet after a winter storm in 1851 and he sounded the new bar in his dory and drew a chart of the hazard. In that same year, after an accident aboard his schooner forced him to temporarily stay ashore, he began an extensive charting of the waters around Monomoy. With his young son as an assistant, Captain Eldridge took a sextant, sounding leads, and other necessary tools and sailed his small schooner *Peri* to different spots off Chatham, including Pollock Rip Shoal, Bearse's Shoal, Stone Horse Shoal, Shovelful Shoal, and Handkerchief Shoal. In these areas, he took soundings and made accurate charts of the locations of these hazards. He also noted the bottom composition in those areas, a factor critical to setting an anchor.

In 1854, after almost five years of work, he published his first pilotage book, *Eldridge's Pilot for Vineyard Sound and Monomoy Shoals*. It was 32 pages and included specific narratives about the dangers of the Monomoy passage, as well as a number of charts that featured compass courses and distances to various navigation landmarks. The book met with instant success and Captain Eldridge, now known as "Chart George," decided to devote himself full time to producing what later became an indispensable resource for mariners. Around this time Eldridge began to have his charts published by Samuel Thaxter & Son of Boston.

Captain Eldridge's son, George Washington Eldridge, had grown up watching his father put together the charts of Nantucket Sound. Father and son had camped together at Monomoy Point,

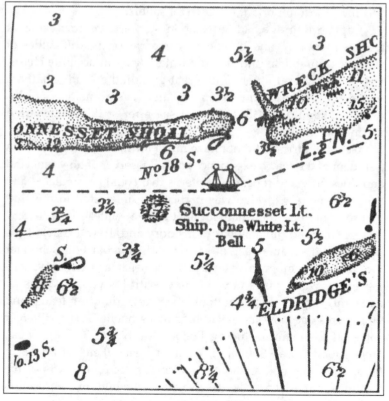

Succonnesset Light Ship, off Cotuit. (Cape Cod Community College)

using it as a base while compiling the information for the first piloting book. While still a teenager, George the younger became a valuable assistant to his father in distributing the piloting book to passing ships around the Sound. At one point, Captain Eldridge asked his son to go to Vineyard Haven and hawk the book to the many ships that took temporary anchorage there while awaiting favorable winds and tides. Seeing a demand for knowledge about how and when the local tide would set, the son began to compile his own tables on the current flow between Vineyard Haven and Woods Hole. At the same time, "Chart George" began to work out the tide tables for a number of other critical shipping lanes along the east coast, including such places as both Chesapeake and Delaware bays, Long Island Sound, Boston Harbor, and even as far south as St. Augustine, Florida.

In 1875, the Eldridges published the first Tide-Book, which allowed sailors to know when and from what direction the tide would turn on a specific day. Such information saved valuable time and allowed mariners to avoid being pushed into hazardous waters by adverse tidal currents. The Tide-Book was later improved to include additional narrative information to assist seamen in avoiding the most treacherous shoal areas.

The genius of Captain George Eldridge was eventually recognized at a World Geographical Congress in Berlin in 1880. With the charts of all nations on display, those of Captain Eldridge won the Gold Medal for accuracy and innovation. George W. Eldridge continued to publish the Tide-Book after his father's death at age 79 in 1900. In 1914, he turned the management of the publication over to his son-in-law, Wilfred O. White, whose family continues to publish the Tide-Book today.

Mariners of all types, from those on oceangoing tankers and tugboat masters to weekend yachtsmen, continue to reach for what is simply referred to as "the Eldridge" when approaching shoal waters. The familiar yellow backed guide, now a staple of mariners, is still a very important tool in the safe navigation of any coastal area.

Chapter 7
And Upon the Sandy Soil

While some went off to sea to find adventure, others made their mark upon the sandy soil. From a bedeviled minister's wife to a stuttering man, and from a simple farmer tending his livestock to a misled jail warden in search of riches, it all points to tales of a local variety.

Barnabas and Remember

Windswept moors mark the landscape of the lower Cape with hillocks sculpted and tree branches twisted by salt breezes. Tales centuries old sprinkled with generous doses of folklore exist in this realm of sky and sand and sea. Such tales can be found in the book *The Narrow Land*, written in the 1930's by Elizabeth Reynard. Within its pages is the tale of a "young theologian" named Barnabas, a Harvard graduate who, with his wife Remember, arrived at Nauset in the early years of the 18th century. The local minister was getting up in years and it was believed the young minister would be his replacement. Yet, powerful forces were at hand.

Folklore tells that Remember owned a fiddle—a fiddle that would lead to mischief and eventually, to murder. According to Reynard, "Never a psalm tune slipped along the bright strings of the fiddle." One day as Barnabas returned home after ministering to the ill he could hear a fiddle playing. As he neared the house he looked in a window to find his new bride inside dancing to a tune played by a visiting sailor. But when Barnabas burst through the door Remember was alone. Later that evening Barnabas broke the devilish fiddle into small pieces.

A number of times, when returning home from ministering, Barnabas was certain he heard the fiddle playing. According to

The Narrow Land, the minister said, "Wife, give to me that Instrument of Satan" to which his wife responded, "'Tis only the sin that sings in thy soul."

So bothersome became the phantom fiddling that Barnabas had a new house built with bars over the windows. Remember became a prisoner in her own home, where she was confined for three years. Despite these measures, Barnabas continued to hear the fiddle playing as he returned home at the end of each day. Yet, when he opened the door he would find Remember alone, and the fiddle was nowhere to be found.

The minister could no longer take his wife's perceived evil ways. In a fit of anger he murdered her and set the house afire. The sound of fiddling could still be heard above the flames. That same evening Barnabas entered Higgins Tavern in Orleans (Eastham) where he wrote out his confession of the murder. He then went out to the aptly named Minister's Pond to drown himself.

Why Wren?
Arguably, one of the most picturesque village scenes on Cape Cod is of Sandwich center and Shawme Pond, with the antique Dexter gristmill in the foreground and the towering spire of the First Church of Christ in the background. Yet embedded within this classic image of a New England village is something rather Olde English. It is the magnificent spire of the church that holds the English element, and in fact its design is associated with a particular Englishman—Sir Christopher Wren—prompting some to nickname the structure, the "Wren Church."

Wren himself was born in East Knoyle, Wiltshire, England in 1632, the son of a clergyman. A remarkably intelligent youngster, Wren excelled in mathematics and the sciences, and was recognized as a prodigy. By the age of 14 he was studying at Wadham College, and by his early 20's he was considered an important English mathematician, scientist, and astronomer. As he reached his late 20's he turned his attention to architecture.

Completing his first project, the Pembroke College Chapel, while only in his early 30's, Wren quickly became regarded as England's foremost architectural designer. So, when part of London burned in 1666, he was charged with the task of overseeing the rebuilding of the affected neighborhoods. It would become a lifetime job, for out of this assignment came the design of more than 50 churches, including his masterpiece—Saint Paul's Cathedral.

Work commenced on St. Paul's in 1675 and continued for the next 35 years. Since Wren lived into his nineties, he was able to see the project reach its fruition. When he died in 1723, he was fittingly buried at the cathedral, which became his monument.

Wren's connection to the Sandwich church stems from the fact that its steeple design closely mirrors a similar spire of one of the master architect's churches in London. In 1848, when the Sandwich church was constructed, Isaac Melvin, a Cambridge, Massachusetts architect, used the Wren design for the 130-foot tower. And therein lies the connection between a Cape Cod church and an English knight.

Christopher Wren never visited Sandwich. Nor, as far as anyone knows, did Elvis Presley. But just as Wren is at least indirectly connected with the classic church in this historic Cape Cod village,

Sandwich's First Church of Christ with her Christopher Wren-inspired steeple. (Jack Sheedy photo)

so also is the King of Rock and Roll. When Elvis released his 1967 Grammy Award winning gospel album *How Great Thou Art*, the jacket cover shows him in a light blue suit in front of a white church. That church is none other than the First Church of Christ in Sandwich. And while one of the songs on that LP was "Crying in the Chapel," Elvis shed no tears in the Cape's oldest town.

Captain Solomon Attaquin's Hotel

Built as a private home in 1840 by sea captain Solomon Attaquin, a Mashpee Indian, Hotel Attaquin on the shores of Mill Pond attracted an impressive clientele. Included were such notables as US Secretary of State Daniel Webster, President Grover Cleveland, and 19th century stage actor Joseph Jefferson. Sadly, the record of these names and of those others who frequented the hotel was perhaps forever lost when the hotel's register went missing around 1910. (Who knows, it may someday turn up in an antiques shop!)

The hotel, described as an "excellent inn" by one 19th century magazine, was indeed frequented by all manner of hunter and fisherman as it was close to Mashpee's teeming lakes and forests. Resting along what is today Route 130, the hotel sat nearby a herring run that connected to Mashpee Lake, one of the largest local bodies of inland water. Also nearby was Wakeby Lake; the two bodies of water combining for a total of 700 acres—home to bass, perch, and pickerel. The 130-acre Lowell Holly Reservation—donated in the 1940s by Harvard president Abbott Lawrence Lowell—separates the two bodies of water. This reservation is populated with various varieties of flora, including holly trees, American beech trees, white pine, blueberry, huckleberry, rhododendron, silverrod, and lady slippers. An undisturbed landscape, it is reminiscent of how the area looked centuries ago when Native Indians were its only inhabitants.

Captain Attaquin began his seafaring career at an early age. Born on January 28, 1810 to Ezra and Sarah (Jones) Attaquin in the southwestern section of town, near Waquoit, he was named for his grandfather. His first position at sea was as a cook on a fishing boat working the Grand Banks. He was about 12 years old at the time. Within a couple of years he shipped out on his first whaling voyage. Future journeys took him to European ports. Occasionally he served as mate and master on vessels carrying freight between the ports of Boston and New York. Over the years he worked his way up the nautical ladder to achieve the position of master.

Meanwhile, on land he served as a Mashpee selectman for more than twenty years, occasionally visiting the General Court to speak on behalf of his Native Indian community. In later years he served as town clerk and treasurer. After the incorporation of Mashpee in 1870 he became the town's first postmaster, a position he held until 1889. Described as "well-educated and well-respected," he married Cynthia Conant and fathered two children.

A campaigner for Native American rights, Attaquin died in 1895 at the grand old age of 85 and is buried at the Attaquin Cemetery near Mashpee Pond. After Attaquin's death, his son ran the hotel, serving as a guide to the establishment's many guests. The hotel, which was also known as the Old Indian Hotel, was described in Arthur Wilson Tarbell's 1932 book *Cape Cod Ahoy* as "an unpretentious hostelry now remodeled ... still standing on its original location where the State Road crosses a small stream." Meanwhile, in his 1937 book *Cape Cod Pilot*, Josef Berger stated that "later generations of Attaquins have kept the hotel," though it changed hands during the 1940s. It eventually was destroyed by fire in the mid-1950s.

The First Cape Cod Land Bank

The first Land Bank on Cape Cod was very different from the 1998 legislation that was created by voters to preserve open space. In fact, the first Land Bank was designed for very different reasons.

In the early 18th century, economic development was not restricted by a shortage of land. There was more than enough open space. Instead, it was the lack of reliable currency that held back the growth of businesses on Cape Cod and in the rest of Massachusetts. People had to rely on bartering and paper currency of dubious value. As a result, the economy was unstable and unpredictable. To remedy the situation, the first colonial Land Bank was established in 1730 to issue lines of credit to entrepreneurs, based on property valuation. Those who participated in the Land Bank—and there were a fair number of Cape Codders who did—pledged real estate to receive bank notes. They agreed to pay a 5% interest rate each year on the money that was advanced. Interest payments could be made in goods such as hemp, flax, cast iron, wool, and even cordwood.

In a sense, the colonial Land Bank idea was similar to what would later be tried by the revolutionary government of France in 1790 when it attempted to finance its programs, not on hard currency, but on lines of credit issued on seized lands of the Catholic Church. In both cases, what happened was that each succeeding issuance of new lines of credit depressed the value of the notes that were already in circulation. Eventually, all of the creditors were wiped out. Cape historian Frederick Freeman noted that the Land Bank had the effect of " ... disaffecting the people, alienating neighbors, and threatening to overwhelm posterity with its curse ... "

Recognizing that no real economic progress could ever be made in the colony without a stable currency, the Massachusetts General Court, in concert with the British Parliament, abolished the Land Bank in 1743. An act of Parliament in 1749 appropriated a large sum of silver to be transported to Boston to serve as the basis of the first sound currency in the colony. Several ships arrived in the winter of 1749-1750 with 215 chests of silver, each of which contained a value of about $3,000. Coins were struck and the government declared that as of March 31, 1750 all debts must be paid in hard currency. While some bartering still took place for years afterward, Cape Codders and the rest of Massachusetts at last had a monetary system that worked. The first Land Bank was dead. Sadly, most of its original investors—the ones who had advanced money on the basis of land value—were wiped out.

Today, of course, the Land Bank assesses owners an additional amount on their property taxes to guarantee that open land is preserved for posterity. Far from having too much land and too little money in circulation, as was the case in the early days of Cape Cod, the exact opposite has come to pass.

The Division of Cape Cod Towns
From the original four towns of Sandwich, Barnstable, Yarmouth, and Eastham, Cape Cod now features fifteen individual townships within Barnstable County. Some of these municipalities came into existence as a natural consequence of geography and settlement

patterns and were the product of harmonious division. Others were born in acrimony and produced hard feelings that lasted for generations. Still others, despite practical arguments and genuine interest, were stillborn and never went beyond the discussion stage, becoming mere footnotes in the Cape's history.

On the Outer Cape, Eastham once held sway over land from Provincetown to Pleasant Bay. Because it was considered "unchurched and ungospelized," as well as being sparsely populated, Chatham couldn't seem to get beyond being categorized as simply a "place" for years. Though it acted, for practical purposes, as a town as early as 1691, sending representatives to the General Court, it was only after securing a permanent minister that it was recognized officially in 1712.

Orleans separated peacefully from Eastham in 1797. Truro, which was incorporated in 1709 from Eastham, included Provincetown for a time until continuous instances of "riotous doings" at "Cape Cod," the name by which it was known, made the town decide that it should end ties with the district. Provincetown, almost like an unwanted child, thus was born in 1727. The upper Cape also experienced division. Falmouth, largely settled by disaffected Barnstable and Sandwich Quakers, became a town in 1686. After getting some autonomy in the 1830's, the former Indian reservation at Marshpee became fully independent in 1870. Citizens in Sandwich attempted unsuccessfully to split that town on a number of occasions in the 19th century. With the second largest land area in Massachusetts, it was a genuine hardship for citizens in places like Pocasset and Cataumet to travel to Sandwich Center for meetings. In 1860, a vote actually carried the measure for division, but a subsequent special meeting rescinded the action and residents of "West Sandwich" had to wait until 1884 when the town of Bourne was incorporated.

One of the most contentious divisions was Brewster's split from Harwich in 1803. The break up came about largely for social and economic reasons. Most of the wealth was centered in the North Parish and taxpayers in that section bridled at supporting their less wealthy townsmen who resided in the south side. An interesting statistic was cited that of the 15 pleasure carriages in the township, 14 of them were in the North Parish. Conversely, of the town's 15 paupers, 13 resided in the South Parish. The poor side of town claimed it only had a single worthy milk cow! The well-to-do ship masters used their influence in the state legislature to cut themselves loose from their poor southern brethren, who fought a rear guard action to block the split. The new town was named after one of the original Pilgrims, the Reverend William Brewster, who as Henry David Thoreau put it with some sarcasm, "would have surely been forgotten otherwise."

Recognizing that its East Precinct had developed into a self-sufficient community under the spiritual tutelage of the Reverend Josiah Dennis, Yarmouth willingly agreed to a division in 1793 and the division was, as one historian put it, "not in consequence of any disaffection or unfriendly sentiment on the part of one section toward the other." The new town named itself after its faithful pastor. But later, as with Brewster, there were fractious issues between north and south siders. The impetus for further division in Dennis came from those residing in South and West Dennis, which by the mid-19th century had become the more wealthy sections. In 1859 a proposal was drafted to create a new town of South Dennis. Dennis town records reveal that in November of 1860 a vote was taken in the affirmative to divide the town along an east-west line that roughly followed the layout of Old Chatham Road. But before representatives could make their case before the General Court another vote was taken in January of 1861 to keep the town together. Unlike the nation in that fateful year, Dennis stayed united.

Other abortive attempts at splitting separate towns off from existing ones occurred in Barnstable. Between 1837 and 1852 there were a dozen proposals for division. On two occasions less than 40 votes at town meeting were the difference in moving forward. In 1836, a number of residents of South Eastham drew up a petition to be allowed to join the town of Orleans. It was unsuccessful. Even the county has seen efforts to divide it. In 1734, claiming that the distance to travel to Barnstable was too great, the towns of Eastham, Harwich, Chatham, Truro, and Provincetown addressed the General Court, "praying for favors" to be allowed to form a separate "Cape Cod" county. Their efforts too, came to naught.

Occasionally the idea of separation and division still will surface. Cape and Island residents, recognizing what a tax generating entity the area is for the rest of Massachusetts, and how little comes back in the form of state aid, periodically make noises about seceding from the Commonwealth. Many residents wish that the Cape Cod Canal was a political barrier as well as a physical one. A few years ago one of the Islands actually entertained the idea of becoming part of New York! Several "Cod Island Republics" have been floated from time to time. In the 1930's, one such proposal even reached the White House and President Roosevelt sent a letter to backers saying that he hated to think that the many relatives he had on the Cape would soon become foreigners. When no one seemed excited about taking payment for debts with money that said "In Cod We Trust," printed on it, the idea eventually died. There has always been a strong strain of independence in Barnstable's villages and the town continues to see occasional movements to break it up. The most recent was in Cotuit a few years ago where the Cotuit Civic Association made rumblings about seceding from the other six villages.

We can probably figure, however, that as the Cape is laid out today, so it will be in the future. The trend toward division seems to have run its course. There hasn't been a successful secession or split in Massachusetts since Gardner broke away from Ashburnham. And that was way back in 1921.

The Whole Story on Woods Holl

In 1850, Joseph Story Fay, a well-to-do Boston merchant, made a brief stop in Woods Hole to make a ferry boat connection to New Bedford where he was to inspect a whaling ship for possible purchase. The hilly pastures out toward Nobska Point and Little Harbor interested him. After a perambulation of the land around the old Parker farm, Fay declared that he had to have it. A Purchase and Sales Agreement was drawn up and Fay ended up with a nice piece of property where he eventually built a lovely summer home.

From that day until his death in the late 1890's, Joseph Story Fay was a dominant figure in his adopted village and town. He was a generous benefactor, giving land for public parks, forests, and beaches. He also provided sites for the St. Joseph's Catholic church and the Episcopal Church of the Messiah. An avid horticulturist, Fay's gardens were the talk of Woods Hole.

But somewhere along the way, Fay branched off into archaeology and it led him to wonder about the town's ancient history, and in particular about the name of the village that he had come to love. He eventually proposed a theory that the Vikings must have long ago visited Falmouth and he speculated that the name for Woods Hole should really have been Woods Holl. As Fay saw it, the word "hole" was actually a corruption of the Norwegian word "holl" meaning "hill." As Fay studied the rolling landscape around his property, he became convinced that the Vikings would naturally have given the name "holl" to the high ground around Nobska lighthouse. Because the Scandinavians used these high points as navigation references, they must have been "holls," not "holes." And further, Fay figured, true holes like Robinson's and Quick's in the Elizabeth Islands were really passages of water between two land masses. Surprisingly, he didn't seem to equate the similarity of the channel passing between Holmes Hole (Vineyard Haven) and Woods Hole as being anything like them.

Using his prominence as a leading figure in the village, he lobbied the citizens to "correct a long standing error." In 1875, all of the male voters of Woods Hole—except for a single unnamed dissenter—signed a petition asking the post office to change the

When Woods Hole was Woods Holl. (Jim Coogan Photo)

name of the village to Woods Holl. That year, the new name went into effect. In 1879, the keystone of the bridge over the entrance to Eel Pond was inscribed with the name Woods Holl. History, as Fay saw it, had been corrected in stone. A few years later, Fay moved to further support his Viking theory by publishing a small pamphlet entitled "Woods Holl: The Track of the Norseman." It was all pretty convincing.

A bit of grumbling by some of the locals who wanted the old name of their village back would occasionally surface, but Fay's generosity to the town and his popularity made it hard for anyone to challenge him. And, after all, hadn't all but a single person endorsed the name change? It wasn't until after Fay's death in 1897 that anything happened. In October of 1899, when the cornerstone for the new post office was set, the stonemason who was charged with putting the village name on it made a mistake and chiseled in the old name—Woods Hole. Faced with this very visible part of its foundation, the post office changed the name back to Woods Hole. It's been called that ever since.

It's hard to be sure about anything in this story. In concocting and spreading his theory, which has influenced and confused historians to this day, Joseph Story Fay was probably most true to his middle name. It's likely that the Vikings did indeed visit Falmouth way back when. Whatever they called the place, however, has surely been long forgotten in the mists of history. The Norse sagas are vague and no one is really certain where they explored. But it's a pretty good bet that by the actions of that seemingly careless stonemason, we can make a pretty good guess to whom that one dissenting vote in 1875 belonged.

The Warden's Money Pit

It was a warm Monday in May of 1849 when three men got off the train in Sandwich. They arrived from Boston carrying some unusual baggage. One had a pickaxe, another a crow bar, and the third carried a spade. As far as any of the interested people watchers in the depot could see, none of them carried any personal baggage. The trio rented a double-seated wagon, threw their tools into the back, and headed off toward Barnstable Village. Further east on the main road, they branched off toward Osterville.

The apparent leader of this expedition was William Phillips. That he was not all that familiar with where he was taking his two companions was made clear when the wagon stopped at the house of Daniel Sturgis. "What town are we in?" asked Phillips. He was told that he'd reached a section of West Barnstable. "That'll do," he tipped his hat to Sturgis and rejoined his two companions on the wagon. "It's just a few miles from here," he reassured them. "I think I remember some of these landmarks." In fact, Phillips had no idea where he was. He'd never been in that place in his life. But with a confidence that belied his unfamiliarity with the terrain, Phillips led the other two south toward Osterville.

This story really begins with a robbery in Virginia. Phillips had taken a large sum of money out of the bank in Wheeling. He was apprehended in Massachusetts and was confined in the jail at Charlestown. While there, Phillips told an inmate a story about burying $50,000 in gold on Cape Cod. He explained that once free, he was planning to go back and dig it up. The story got back to the Warden of the prison, a man by the name of Robinson. Thinking he might be able to make a deal with Phillips, he suggested to the prisoner that, in exchange for details about the buried treasure life in jail could be made a good deal better than it presently was. Phillips was amenable to providing information about the whereabouts of the gold, but told the Warden that he would have to go with him to Cape Cod because he had not written down a map for fear it would fall into the wrong hands. "I'll recognize the spot when I see it," he told the Warden.

Robinson brought a third man into the scheme. He was the Charlestown City Marshall and his name was Nichols. With Phillips as their guide, Nichols and Robinson had boarded the morning train for the Cape. Around 2:00 p.m., the three were in a remote area between Cotuit and Marstons Mills. "This is it," Phillips pointed. "Over in that hollow just up from the shore. I remember that house just back there." The three men piled out of the wagon and began digging in the sandy soil.

The house nearby was that of Alexander Scudder and as dusk cut short their efforts, the members of the expedition knocked on his door, asking for lodging for the night. The men requested that they all be in the same room. They wanted it locked and lighted throughout the night. And they asked to have their breakfast brought up to them at first light. They passed the night deep in golden dreams.

The next morning, the trio was back digging. They took turns at the labor. At this point the pit was about four feet across and five feet deep. It was difficult to keep the sides from collapsing in the sandy soil. By 10:00 a.m. the hole was a good seven feet deep and it took a hand from above to bring the digger up from the bottom. "We are really close now," said Phillips. "The chest should be in view any minute." Eager to be the first to hear the clunk of spade on wood, Nichols volunteered to take the next shift. He got down and began to shovel with great speed. Warden Robinson crouched at the edge of the pit waiting for his partner to strike the treasure. Phillips gave Robinson a good shove from behind and the Warden went into the pit on top of Nichols. The convict was off through the woods like a shot as the two officials tried to untangle themselves and get out of the hole. A witness later recalled seeing a lone man headed across some fields, "with telegraphic rapidity" while throwing an occasional glance over his shoulder. As one news report suggested, Phillips "was making the most of his newly acquired freedom, and enlarging its area with all his might."

Nichols and Robinson eventually got out of the pit and took the wagon back to Sandwich. While waiting at the depot for the Boston train, they answered no questions about where their other companion was and, in fact, seemed not to want to make any conversation at all. In less than a week, however, the story was all over the city about how the prisoner Phillips had hoodwinked two officials in a clever escape plan. The Warden and the Marshall were the butt of numerous jokes about their "Cape Cod Gold Mine." About three months later, Phillips was recaptured in the Boston area. Because the wily and creative convict had provided the city with some laughs at the expense of two of the state's important law enforcement officials, a newspaper reflected "there was a strong feeling of regret manifested yesterday when his recapture became known."

The Stuttering Man and the Dead Horse
There's an old story that has its roots in Yarmouth around the beginning of the 20th century. Like most stories, it has been

embellished and tweaked over the years and, in its various forms, it could probably be told in just about any town in New England.

A Yarmouth man was reading the weekly copy of the *Cape Cod Item* and he happened to see an advertisement for a horse auction to be held in Boston the following week. He had need of a good horse and so, on the appointed date, he took himself to the Yarmouth Depot and boarded the morning train for the city. Arriving in plenty of time, he got to the fairgrounds where the horse auction was to be held and he had a chance to look at some of the animals that were going to be for sale. There was one in particular that he liked and he set himself to see if he could get it.

The auction started about 11:00 in the morning and when the Cape man's horse came on the block, he opened the bidding at $10.00. Another man had an interest in the same horse and the bidding went up—$15.00, $20.00, and then $30.00. When the price reached $35.00, the competitor dropped out and the Yarmouth man was declared the owner of the horse. He was told that he could make arrangements to have it shipped home after lunch and that he could see the animal at a stable about a half-mile from the fairground.

Our Cape Codder was hungry and as he looked for a restaurant, the man who had been bidding against him sidled up and suggested they have lunch together. While eating, the man mentioned that he was from Springfield and was staying at the Quincy House Hotel for a couple of days. He told the Yarmouth man to come by and have a drink after making the arrangements for the horse to be shipped home. The evening train to Cape Cod left at 5:30 p.m. so there wouldn't be any problem. They shook on it and the Yarmouth man headed over to the stable to see his horse.

Arriving at the stable, the purchaser was told that the animal was out back down a row of stalls. When he got to the stall and looked in, he saw that the horse was dead. Thinking quickly, he went back over to the hotel where his competitor was staying. "I've just received a telegram," he told his new friend. "My wife has taken very ill and I must get back to Cape Cod right away. I didn't have time to deal with the horse." He suggested that if the man from Springfield still wanted the horse, he'd sell it to him for the same $35.00 bid price. "Seems fair enough," said the man and they shook on it.

As he walked quickly toward South Station, the Yarmouth man was very nervous. He was certain that someone would find out about the dead horse and that he would be arrested. He finally got to the station and found a long line of people waiting for tickets. He became ever more nervous as he looked over his shoulder toward the street. The 5:30 train was the last one to leave for the Cape that day. If he didn't get on it, he'd be stuck in Boston for the night. By the time he got to the ticket window, he was sweating and had begun to stutter.

"Give. . Gi. . Give me a tic, . . tick,. . ticket to Yar, . .Yar., Yar. ." He could not get the sentence out. And it seemed that "Yarmouth" had become an impossible tongue twister.

The clerk was becoming impatient as the agitated man struggled with stating his destination. Finally, in desperation, he blurted out, "Oh, forget it. Give me a ticket to South Dennis and I'll walk home."

Provincetown's Human Fly

It was a warm and comfortable night in Provincetown on July 22, 1959 when 21-year old Jonathan Thomas secured his place in Cape Cod history. Apparently on a dare, the young Cape-tip native decided to climb the 252-foot Pilgrim Monument—on the outside.

Undoubtedly fueled by some sort of liberating spirits, Thomas showed no fear as he successfully scaled the granite structure, moving hand over foot up the lightning rod on the sheer face of the southern wall. Everything seemed to be fine until he got to the observation area of the structure, about 225 feet up. At this point he realized that the windows had iron bars welded across them and he could not get inside. The idea of climbing back down was not appealing. Immediately sobered by his predicament, Thomas began yelling for help.

The local police department was alerted and about 2:00 a.m. Sergeant Francis Marshall (later chief of the Provincetown Police Department), together with patrolmen Donald Gleason and William Silva, were able to cut through the bars with a hacksaw supplied by local taxi operator John Gonsalves, and haul Mr. Thomas to safety feet first through the opening. He had been stuck outside for more than two hours.

The next morning Thomas appeared in front of Special Justice
Leo P. Doherty in Second District Court to answer a charge of
disturbing the peace and trespassing. He pleaded guilty and was
fined $28.00 for his unauthorized climb.

The story should have ended there but it did not. Jonathan
Thomas eventually moved from the Cape tip to New Hampshire.
His exploit of that July night became part of the folklore of
Provincetown. Eighteen years after his notorious and dangerous
climb, Thomas was doing some repair work on his house in New
Hampshire. While shingling the roof, he lost his balance and fell 16
feet to his death. He was 39 years old.

Chapter 8
Cape Codders at Play

Though most days it was hard work from dawn to dusk, on other days Cape Codders were able to enjoy a little recreation in their daily lives. Native Indians even found time for friendly competition. Over the years, the Cape has been home to baseball, ice hockey, basketball, wrestling, and of course, the County Fair.

Shinney and La Crosier
Some may believe that sport is something that was developed in recent centuries by "modern" peoples. This is perhaps true of some sports, such as football, which is truly a 20th century game. But other sporting events go back a number of centuries and involved people we could scarcely call "modern."

Perhaps the most widely known games played by ancient people involved the sporting events associated with the Olympics of the ancient Greeks. A handful of today's Olympic events, such as wrestling, javelin, and the marathon, can be traced back to these original games. The Romans had their own games, as evidenced by their arenas, most notably the Colosseum. It would seem their games had less to do with sportsmanship and cultural awareness and more to do with pitting slave against slave in some sort of gladiatorial event.

Yet, we don't necessarily have to go back to ancient Greece or Rome to find the root of some of the games played here in this country. In fact, we don't even need to leave our shores. The earliest explorers to this hemisphere were the first to witness the Natives engaging in various forms of sport. Typically, the games were held to honor some major event in their society, like the annual harvest of crops or the fall hunt. These Native "harvest homes" were times of great celebration, a time to thank their gods for the abundant harvest, and a time to celebrate themselves.

Many times, competitions were held between two or more tribes in order to strengthen their bonds of friendship. Sporting events might include wrestling, foot races, canoe races, swimming races, and a number of games of marksmanship. Shooting arrows or throwing darts at a target were popular competitions, as were other accuracy events such as throwing spears at a rolling wooden hoop or casting a javelin to land closest to a particular target. Stones and heavy rocks were tossed for distance, like a shot put.

There were also team sports, such as tug-of-war, "shinney," and "baggatiewag." Shinney was similar to field hockey, with team members using a wooden stick to strike a ball made of either wood or animal skin. The objective was to hit the ball into the opponent's territory and perhaps into some type of goal area. It's interesting that the game was called "shinney," for in modern field hockey the shins of the participants can take an awful beating!

Baggatiewag, on the other hand, is the predecessor to lacrosse. Using a stick with a bag of rawhide at the end, the Natives passed a ball of animal skin back and forth until the teammates reached the opponent's goal as designated by a wooden post. French explorers who witnessed the game of baggatiewag being played claimed that the playing field was at least a mile long. To the French the sticks used resembled a bishop's staff (or "crosier"), so they called the game la crosier, which later became "lacrosse."

A Card Game Interrupted
On the breezy autumn evening of October 22, 1827, the regulars shuffled into Crocker Tavern along the main street in Barnstable Village. According to Josiah Hinckley, one of a handful of young local men playing cards at the tavern that evening, it was "blowing almost a gale." Playing cards with Hinckley was Captain Joseph Bursley. Little did the men know that their friendly game of cards would be interrupted by an event that continues to impact the residents of Barnstable County even today—nearly 200 years later.

Across the street stood the County House, home to the Registry of Deeds, the Clerk of Courts, and the Probate Office. These offices held irreplaceable Cape Cod records dating back to the time of settlement. Nearing eleven o'clock, with the card game still in progress, "the knocker on the front door was put into rapid motion, attended with the cry of fire," according to Hinckley as written in historian Donald Trayser's book *Barnstable: Three Centuries of a Cape Cod Town*. Reverend Henry Hersey of the local east parish had noticed flames coming from the County House and afterwards recorded his actions: "...at 15 minutes before 11 o'clock I discovered the county house to be on fire and gave the alarm."

Card players Hinckley and Bursley sprang to action, assisted by Rev. Hersey and an Isaac Chipman. Entering the building via the front door, they managed to save probate records by passing them through an open window. Once finished with probate, they attempted to move on to other parts of the building, but the smoke was too thick. By then, more villagers appeared on the scene to offer assistance. Hinckley and Bursley tried to make their way to the Registry of Deeds on the second floor, but the smoke prevented them. So, they decided to make another attempt from outside the building. Someone rounded up a ladder and Hinckley climbed to the window above where he kicked in the glass. With fresh oxygen, the fire grew in intensity, preventing Hinckley from entering. He managed to reach inside the window and save a lone volume of deeds before escaping the flames. Ninety-three other volumes were lost, thus destroying land records centuries old. Records of the Clerk of Courts were also destroyed. Such a devastating loss of information and irreplaceable local history has forever left a void in Barnstable's past and has raised questions over past property ownership. It is why the majority of land deeds are of the quitclaims variety.

And further, it is not known whether the card game at Crocker Tavern was ever resumed.

Horse Racing at "Witchmere" Harbor?

When Cape Cod's master mariners returned to this sandy fishhook of land for a couple of months of relaxation before the seas called to them again, they typically found their way down to the local racetrack to wager some of the money they had earned upon their last successful voyage. It was a gentlemanly way to spend a Saturday afternoon.

During the latter half of the 19th century, horse racing became a popular form of entertainment, not only for sea captains, but also for local fishermen and farmers, and anyone with a taste for the track and a small bit of money to wager. Tracks could be found in a number of Cape locations, such as at West Dennis where the half-mile Riverside Trotting Park rested near the banks of Swan River. Designed by sea captain David Fisk, Riverside boasted grandstands to hold more than two hundred spectators, as well as a judge's stand and a tank to water the racehorses. Twenty-five cents was the cost of admission.

In his book *Barnstable: Three Centuries of a Cape Cod Town*, historian Donald G. Trayser states that, "Nearly all the villages of Barnstable had their trotting parks about this time," referring to the year 1876. Hundreds of spectators could be expected to turn out at the Hyannis Trotting Park on Saturdays, with that number swelling to a thousand or more during the summer. The Barnstable fairgrounds on the north side of town was also the site of a horse racing track, located at the Agricultural Hall—the site of the annual County Fair.

Falmouth had a 200-yard track off Gifford Street that typically attracted more than one thousand spectators on race day. The 24-acre complex had a track made of clay and buildings to house the horses. The purse could run into thousands of dollars—a sizeable amount in those days.

Harwichport had a racetrack built around a circular pond located on Nantucket Sound. Author Josef Berger, in his book *Cape Cod Pilot*, wrote, "When the houses along shore began to fill up with retired skippers, these old men built a racetrack around the pond and set out after each other in their sulkies as they once had done aboard their vessels." Another New England historian, Edward Rowe Snow, added: "… it was the custom for the old sea captains to race their horses around this fresh water pond in Harwichport, and there were many thrilling encounters in which as much as fifty bushels of oats was the gambling stake."

But Snow's account of the Harwichport racetrack provides more to the story, including the opinion of the local ladies of the village and what they thought of the events that went on there. The women frowned on the activities, sensing that devilishness abounded, and they set out to put an end to the tomfoolery. It seems that in addition to racing and gambling, a hotel next to the track was a den of iniquity where "activities of various and sundry nature were said to have taken place." Interestingly, the hotel eventually burned and interest in horse racing in Harwichport waned. A proposal to break through the short distance from the pond to Nantucket Sound, and thus create a saltwater harbor, met with a favorable response. Today that body of water is known as Wychmere Harbor ... although Snow claims that once the harbor was known as "Witchmere," perhaps remembering the "devilish" activities that once went on at the hotel along its shore.

Nowadays, the racetracks are gone, their only reminders being streets named Trotting Park Road located in such places as West Dennis, Falmouth, and on the Barnstable/Sandwich line. Yet, with a little imagination, one can stand on the bluff overlooking Wychmere Harbor and almost see the horses racing below.

Barnstable County Fair
Even though Cape Cod of old was a peninsula of seafarers, it was also populated by local farmers who cultivated their fields and raised livestock. Family farms dotted the landscape, and even as recently as the 20th century the Cape displayed an agrarian persona. As such, the locals were in touch with the changing seasons, from spring planting to summer's growth, and from the fall harvest to winter's silent chill. And then the cycle began anew.

In May 1843, the Barnstable County Agricultural Society was formed and the next year the first agricultural fair was held after the harvest on the grounds of Barnstable village's County Courthouse. Like most county fairs of that age, the event featured prize-winning crops, livestock displays, and craft exhibits. Following fairs took place at the 30-acre Barnstable Agricultural Society grounds along today's Route 6A in Barnstable village, although two 19th century fairs were held elsewhere (in 1851 at Orleans and the following year at Sandwich).

With each new year came a bigger and better fair. Exhibits were held in the Agricultural Hall building, while horse races took place on a new track built in 1860. There were also oxen pulls, salt hay stacking competitions, performances on stage, sideshow events, baseball games, and of course, plenty of food. By the turn of the 20th century the fair drew about 12,000 attendees, with the trotting races and baseball championship serving as big draws.

In her book *Horse and Buggy Days on Old Cape Cod*, Hattie Blossom Fritze, who was a teenager at the turn of the century, described the annual County Fair as follows: "The Barnstable County Fair was, in my youth, quite the most important event of the year. People from all over the Cape came to the fairground, located on what is now Bacon Farm. I can well imagine what it must have meant to the small boys of the neighborhood. How they would sneak out at dawn to arrive first and get whatever job awaited around the big animal tents or the trotting horses' quarters."

Her reminisces continue: "There were three days of the fair, the middle one being Governor's Day, when either he or a representative would usually show up ... It seemed that just about everyone we knew attended and there was a regular old home week celebration, with much hand shaking and renewing of old acquaintances."

After World War I the fair was still going strong as reported in a 1919 issue of the *Barnstable Patriot*: "This is a gala week for Barnstable County ... Features galore are the order of the day. With the horse show, dog show, band concerts, vaudeville performances, added to the regular exhibits of vegetables, fruits, flowers, food, handmade household and fancy articles, cattle, poultry, etc., there is never a dull moment at the fair." The annual fair continued to attract large crowds into the 1920's, but during the latter part of the decade there was a steady decline in interest. By 1932, with the Great Depression hovering over the local economy, the agricultural society was dissolved. Meanwhile, Joseph Berger, author of *Cape Cod Pilot*, wrote in 1937: "There will never be another County Fair in Barnstable, at least none under the auspices of the Society."

With the Town of Barnstable's 1939 tercentenary celebration the Barnstable County Fair was suddenly, though briefly, resurrected. The event retreated back into its state of hibernation for more than a decade until a three-day August event was held in Marstons Mills (near the present golf course) in 1954. Supplementing the usual livestock exhibits, stage performances, and baseball games were circus acts and even a dance competition. Though the fair was considered a success, Hattie Blossom Fritze wrote in her book, "A few years ago, a new Fair was started near Marstons Mills, but it does not have the glamour of the old one." Despite ups and downs, the fair survived into the mid-1970's when the location was changed to Route 151 in North Falmouth, where it is currently held. Today the fair takes place in late July with 4-H displays, horse shows, horticultural displays, a petting zoo, farmyard shows, stage performances, and the midway. Now more than a century and a half old, the annual County Fair hearkens back to the Cape's proud agrarian roots.

A Cape Cod Family That Brought Culture to Chicago

In the decades before the Civil War, many Cape Codders saw the sea as the best opportunity for wealth and fortune. The age of the legendary "Blue Water Men" began in this time period. Whalers, clipper ship captains, and merchant sailors, along with other enterprising men, traveled across the world and came back rich men. When gold was discovered in California, there was further stimulus to leave Cape Cod and head west. But some individuals saw economic opportunity a bit closer than the Golden State and it did not necessitate going to sea. Along with a number of other local entrepreneurs, members of Brewster's Crosby family made the move to Chicago, Illinois and for them, it paid off handsomely.

Albert Crosby was the first in his family to transfer his interests from Cape Cod to Chicago, arriving in the mid-western city in 1848 where he opened a business dealing in liquor and tea. The city then had less than twenty-five thousand people and was still essentially a frontier town with not a single paved street. But business was good and within a year Albert encouraged his uncle Isaac and his father Nathan to come west and join him in a distillery partnership. Other family members from Brewster that arrived in the city around that time were Charles Crosby, Rowland Crosby, and Albert's 19-year old younger cousin Uranus Crosby. From the start, the family business enterprise, Albert Crosby & Co., was successful, riding the rapid growth and thirsty appetite of the windy city.

When the Republican Party convention was held in Chicago in the fall of 1860, Albert Crosby & Co. was the major liquor supplier for the politicians who held their caucus parties around the Wigwam convention center. Against the backdrop of impending civil war, the Crosbys learned from Washington insiders that if war should come, the federal government would be imposing a hefty liquor tax to finance it. With this knowledge, the Crosbys began to stockpile large amounts of pre-tax liquor in their warehouses. When war did come, and the government imposed the tax, the Crosbys were able to undersell the market. Their profits were enormous.

Another family member arrived in 1861. Chatham-born Samuel Mayo Nickerson was related to the Crosbys on his mother's side and had also married Matilda Crosby, a cousin. He started his own liquor business, S.M. Nickerson & Co., which in 1862 was renamed the North Branch Distilling Co. With a growing market for their product, all of these Cape Cod men became wealthy. Nickerson used his profits to charter the First National Bank of Chicago. Eventually he became the bank's president.

Perhaps the most interesting member of the group was Uranus Crosby. Only peripherally interested in the distillery business, Uranus fancied himself an art lover and a man of high culture. He could see little of any refinement in his adopted city. Already a wealthy man by his early 30's, Uranus threw himself into seeing that Chicago would have its own first class opera house. He traveled to Italy in 1863 to view some of the best examples of such venues and returned with a set of plans guaranteed to make Chicago the equal of any of the more cultured cities of the east coast. He put up his personal fortune of a half million dollars and construction began in 1864.

It was clear from the beginning that Uranus had underestimated how much his vision was going to cost. With the building only half finished, he approached Samuel Nickerson's bank for an additional loan of $250,000. Cousin Sam Nickerson had doubts about the viability of the enterprise. But he extended the funds when Uranus told him that the opera house would also feature a major art gallery—something close to both Nickerson and his wife's hearts. Construction went forward and the magnificent building was completed in April of 1865.

There was still the question as to whether Chicagoans would support grand Italian opera. When Verdi's *Il Traviatore* opened to packed audiences it seemed that Uranus had been right. But after the initial wave of enthusiasm, the opera house had difficulty bringing in enough patrons to pay its bills. As an inexperienced impresario, Uranus was a poor contract negotiator. There were many empty dates, margins were tight, and the building was often closed. Family members encouraged Uranus to hire some vaudeville and burlesque shows to fill his open dates and to bring in more patrons, but Uranus refused to book what he termed "common entertainments." Ever the purist, he stayed with classical opera performances throughout the first season.

As the spring of 1866 approached, Uranus was near bankruptcy. Creditors held title to the building and it looked like he would lose everything. Again, he went to his cousin Sam Nickerson. Fearful of pouring good money after bad, but looking to salvage his bank's interest in the property, Nickerson and the board of directors came up with the scheme of essentially raffling off the opera house by selling lottery tickets. Lotteries were illegal, but Nickerson knew that city officials would look the other way if it were pitched as a support of the arts program. To skirt the law, all ticket purchasers were guaranteed something of value as a prize. A proviso was also added that the winner would have to keep the Crosby name on the building and Uranus would be able to stay as manager.

Two hundred thousand tickets were printed, to be sold at $5.00 each. The date of the drawing was scheduled for January 21, 1867. There was an enthusiasm like the city had never seen before.

Albert Crosby's Brewster mansion, Tawasentha. (Cape Cod Community College)

Tickets were advertised nationwide and sales were brisk from New Orleans to Montreal. By the late fall, the take had reached almost a million dollars. When the date of the drawing came, Chicago came to a standstill. At noon on the 21st, the drawing began with the first 300 tickets taking pieces of artwork from the Crosby gallery. At 2:20 p.m. the final drawing for the opera house itself was made. There was a hush in the building and in the street outside. Telegraph operators stood by across the country. "58600!! is the winning ticket!!" shouted the judge, who held it up before the crowd. There was no immediate claimant. Since the tickets did not have the name of the purchaser written on them, it took time to go back to the sales books to find who held the winner.

It turned out that a rural mill owner, Abraham Lee of Randolph County, Illinois, had purchased the winning ticket. When he arrived in Chicago a week later, he quickly went to the opera house to present it. He told the lottery officials that he wanted to sell the building. Without any additional bidding, the organizers settled on paying Lee $200,000. As he emerged from the building he spread his arms and told people waiting outside, "I owned all of this for a half hour!" He got into a coach, headed for the railroad station and was gone.

Many considered what had happened to be an outrage. Losers felt they had been swindled. People wondered if Abraham Lee had been in on it. Negative sentiment increased when it was learned that almost 25,000 tickets had not been sold and remained in the control of lottery organizers. Several of the most expensive pieces of artwork, including the second prize painting, had gone to those tickets. But for Uranus Crosby everything had come up roses. The net from ticket sales was enough to pay off all creditors and leave him with his building and almost $300,000.

The Crosby family in Chicago had become prominent enough that the backlash over the opera house lottery stood to hurt them financially and socially. Facing threats of lawsuits, Uranus reluctantly sold his interest in the opera house to his cousin Albert and removed himself from active management of the enterprise. With a new manager, the opera house began to prosper. Albert Crosby apparently had no problems with what some critics described as "cheap tinsel" and the "leg business." With a mix of burlesque and opera the enterprise stayed in the black for several seasons. But there was increasing faultfinding in the newspapers that the building had become a "house of assignation" and even worse— "a den of prostitution."

In 1871, the opera house was given a major overhaul. Uranus, who had remained behind the scenes after the lottery embarrassment, reemerged as a full partner with his cousin. He invested heavily in the renovations. The opera house was scheduled for a grand reopening in October, but Fate intervened and the great Chicago fire of October 7, 1871 completely destroyed the building and everything around it. On the morning of October 10th, as the cousins surveyed the ruins, there was nothing left but a pile of charred bricks and stone. The building, incredibly, was not insured.

Albert Crosby suffered great losses in the fire. Many of his buildings were in ruins. But he rebuilt his fortune with investments in railroads and breweries. He never, however, apparently satisfied all of his creditors. In 1877, with a new and much younger wife, he abruptly left Chicago for Europe to spend the better part of a decade living the high life abroad. In 1887, the couple returned to Brewster and built an extravagant Romanesque-style home around the old family cottage. Albert called it "Tawasentha." But even in the remoteness of this sleepy Cape town his Chicago creditors eventually found him. All his remaining fortune was used to satisfy his debts. At the same time, his first wife instituted a nasty divorce suit and Crosby was forced to declare bankruptcy in 1889. He died in Brewster in 1906 at age 83.

And what of Uranus Crosby who had been at the center of it all? He left Chicago after the fire with just the clothes on his back. He went home to Brewster and moved in with his parents, continuing to live quietly in the family home after their deaths. The former "Beau Brummell" of Chicago became one of Brewster's solid and well liked citizens and a member of the First Parish Church where he held office. In March of 1903, his final act over, he died with both his cousins, Sam Nickerson and Albert Crosby, by his side.

Interlaken
Cape Cod is certainly well known as a summer resort, but it may come as a surprise to some that more than a century ago there was

a pretty good market here for winter tourism as well. Ice-skating and ice boating brought in many people to Pleasant Lake in Harwich. Each winter the village would make a temporary change to its name, calling itself "Interlaken." It was a good name considering the nearness of Long Pond, Pleasant Lake, and Bangs Pond. The village between the lakes took on aspects of a mini-Tyrolean village. Special trains were chartered to bring in groups of skaters on weekends.

Most old timers will tell you that winters on Cape Cod used to be a lot colder in earlier days. Indeed, a review of newspapers from the late 19th century and even into much of the 20th century will confirm this. Sub-zero temperature readings that began in December and "four quilt nights" went right along with the annual fall gathering of seaweed to "bank up" the foundations of houses to withstand the cold. Ice in the ponds went as thick as 12 to 14 inches and could last into March. There was a good trade in ice harvesting in every community. Naturally this kind of weather closed down the fisheries and for a couple of months ship owners hauled their vessels for repair.

But living on the Cape in that period was not all work. And in between repairing their boats, there was time for residents to have some recreation. Many of the men, especially those who were sailors, enjoyed ice boating. Fleets of small craft engaged in lively races of up to 60 miles an hour going across these large expanses of frozen water. Captain Alvin Cahoon was perhaps the most well known of these ice yachtsman. He skippered his small "Flying Dragon" to many victories, besting many of his seagoing compatriots. There was even one iceboat built by Nathan Smalley that could carry up to 12 passengers. During January and February, hundreds of spectators came to the lakes to see and participate in the activities. Bonfires and illuminations were part of these winter gatherings. Local people brought their horses and wagons out onto the ice for trotting races. On Wednesday and Saturday evenings, Alexander's Three Piece Band provided entertainment as skaters whirled across the ice in the moonlight.

It was all a romantic and now forgotten time. With warmer winters, it's rare to see much activity on the ice these days. People are more likely now to come to the Cape to languish in a hot tub at a well-appointed resort complex. The railroad to Pleasant Lake is long gone. Still, on the occasional cold starry night, as one stands on the quiet shore of Long Pond not far from the Brewster town line, it's possible to conjure up those evenings of winter fun of long ago.

"Deacon Danny" MacFayden

Baseball started early on Cape Cod and evidence of box scores can be found in local papers as early as the late 1860's. One report of a game in 1879 carried the timeless complaint that "The umpire was troubled with an obliquity of vision." "Town ball," as the early version of the game was known, developed a strong local fan base. With such an interest in the national pastime, it seems strange that only one native-born ball player ever made it to the major leagues for more than a cup of coffee. What is even more unusual is that he played for both professional teams in Boston, the Red Sox and the Braves. He was Daniel Knowles MacFayden of North Truro.

Known as "Deacon" by his teammates, perhaps because as the first professional player to wear glasses in a game he looked like a clergyman, MacFayden undoubtedly got his start in the rough ball field adjacent to the Highland Links Golf Club in North Truro. The son of Walter Knowles MacFayden, he was born in 1905 and lived in a section of the town known as "Bean Hill." By his teens, he'd moved off Cape to Somerville, Massachusetts. There MacFayden pitched for the high school team in that city where he was undefeated for two straight years. In one game that went twelve innings, he struck out 33 players, giving up only four hits.

He was scouted by many professional teams and was signed by the Boston Red Sox. At 21, he pitched in his first big league game and soon after became a regular part of the Sox rotation. MacFayden was known for possessing a mean curve ball and he won 52 games for the BoSox during his stint with them. In 1932, he was traded to the New York Yankees where he stayed for three seasons. In those years his teammates included Babe Ruth and Lou Gehrig in a line-up of sluggers that was called "Murderers Row."

In 1935, MacFayden spent a year with the Cincinnati Reds where he was used sparingly. Back in Boston for the 1936 season,

Truro's major leaguer, "Deacon Danny" MacFayden. (Chuck Myrbeck collection)

"The Deacon" was this time with the National League Braves where he stayed until 1940. His career was over in 1943 after seventeen workmanlike years as a pitcher. His best year in the majors was in 1936 when he won 17 games for the Braves with an earned run average of 2.87. In his career, he won a total of 132 games. Even though his overall winning percentage was less than .500, in today's market numbers like this would have made him a multimillionaire.

After his playing days ended, he became the baseball coach at Bowdoin College in Maine where he won eight state collegiate championships. He died at age 67 on August 26, 1972 in Brunswick, Maine.

When Provincetown Banned Baseball

In the early part of the twentieth century, during the summers the U.S. Navy would bring the big battleships of the North American Squadron into the sea range north of Provincetown for gunnery practice. The fleet often put into Provincetown Harbor on weekends and the sailors would be given liberty. Hundreds of adventurous young men came ashore looking for something to do. In a town that had less than 3,000 people in it, the impact of the bluejacket "invasion" was a mixed blessing.

The merchants liked it, as they were able to sell souvenirs to the sailors. Farmers and fishermen sold fresh produce and fish to the fleet at a nice profit. Restaurants also prospered, serving a group that paid well for home cooked meals, but Provincetown at this time was a "dry" town. The sailors naturally expected that they would have some alcohol to accompany their shore dinners. When they found that they couldn't slack their thirst on anything stronger than root beer, they took matters into their own hands, smuggling liquor into town aboard the railroad train that came several times a day. A number of incidents involving intoxicated sailors prompted the board of selectmen to make a plea to the Squadron Commander, Admiral Robley Evans, to do something to control his men. Evans beefed up his shore patrol and did his best to encourage his sailors to pursue healthy activities, but the incidents continued, as did the complaints of many citizens.

At last, thinking he had a solution, Evans convinced the Navy Department to come up with funds to purchase some land in Provincetown to build an athletic field for the fleet's use. In the summer of 1905, a new baseball field opened with weekend tournaments between ships of the fleet. The games were very popular

Admiral Robley Evans, AKA "Fighting Bob. (U.S. Navy photo)

with both the sailors and the townspeople. Instances of rowdy behavior declined and it seemed that the problem was solved. On both Saturdays and Sundays, large crowds converged on Evans Field, as it was named, where they spent the days watching the ballgames.

There were, however, some people at the Cape tip who were decidedly unhappy with the turn of events. These were the town's clergymen who were experiencing a marked decline in church attendance on Sundays. It seems that the citizens were choosing the national game over religious services. In a private meeting with Provincetown selectmen, the clergymen demanded that the 1692 Massachusetts Blue Laws banning Sunday entertainments and other frivolous activities on the Sabbath be enforced. Without consulting the business community, the selectmen told Admiral Evans that the Sunday ballgames would have to cease because they were an affront to law and order on the Sabbath.

Evans, who believed that he had met the town's complaints about his sailors' behavior more than half way, was very upset. As a compromise, he offered to hold the start of the games until the afternoon, after church services had concluded. But this wasn't enough for the clergymen who demanded a complete ban on any sporting activities on Sunday. When Evans showed a reluctance to comply with their wishes, the clergymen pressured the selectmen into writing a letter to the Secretary of the Navy criticizing the admiral for refusing to comply with the Lord's Day laws.

Admiral Evans, who had earned the nickname "Fighting Bob" during the Spanish American War, abruptly broke off negotiations with the town officials and angrily ordered his fleet out of Provincetown. Saying that he no longer considered Provincetown a suitable liberty port, Evans vowed that he would henceforth take his ships to other New England ports where their economic impact would be better appreciated. When the news broke that there would be no more fleet visits at the Cape tip, most of the citizens—and particularly the merchants—were wild. Thousands of dollars were at stake and the selectmen faced a furious backlash against their hasty actions. There was talk of recalling every one of them.

Throughout the fall and winter of 1905 and 1906, a number of letters went from Provincetown to the Navy Department trying to convince authorities to change Evans' mind. A special town meeting was called and an official letter was drafted apologizing to Admiral Evans and entreating him to bring the fleet back to Provincetown.

But it was too late. "Fighting Bob" was angry enough at what he believed to have been shoddy treatment by town officials and he would not reconsider. During the summer of 1906, the North Atlantic Squadron visited ports such as Rockport, Massachusetts, and Portsmouth, New Hampshire and spent its money away from Provincetown. To compound matters, it seemed that the ships took gunnery practice just a bit closer to the Cape tip than had been the case during previous summers. Houses shook and windows rattled from the concussions during the week but on weekends, Provincetown was deathly quiet. The ban on baseball cost the town dearly.

Admiral Evans eventually retired and relations were smoothed over with his successor. The fleet did return to Provincetown and it continued to use the harbor well into the 1920's. The baseball field was once again used by the sailors on weekends, apparently without complaint by anyone. The ban on baseball was forgotten. In the 1920's, not only was Provincetown a "dry" town, but so also was the entire country. Today, to an observer sitting on a bench in front of the town hall and watching the mix of summer visitors passing by in this most unique of Cape Cod towns, it seems pretty clear that nothing is ever banned at the Cape tip anymore—on Sundays or on any other day of the week!

A Hill, a Mill, and a Wrestling Arena

When the Baxter brothers, John and Shubael, built their water powered grist mill along the county road in West Yarmouth in the early 1700's, they had no idea that this area would one day become the site of a number of entertainment venues and sometimes raucous attractions in the first half of the twentieth century. From circuses and carnivals, to roller-skating and professional wrestling, Mill Hill was the place to be for a good time from the early 1920's through the early 1960's.

Perhaps the first structure that transformed the Mill Hill area into a mecca for young people seeking entertainment was the Mill

Hill Pavilion, which was built in 1916. Lots of young flappers and gentlemen in their flivvers popularized the dance hall with its lively weekend concerts. When the dancers cleared out, the building was used as a roller skating rink. A large tent was set up for beano games with a Friday night "Bank Night" which offered a $50.00 cash prize to the winner. Sometimes the site was the scene of activities that were not so uplifting. In June of 1926, there was a large Ku Klux Klan rally held in the field beside the Pavilion which drew over 1,000 people. One hundred members of the Klan paraded in full regalia.

After the Pavilion burned down in 1928, it was replaced across Route 28 by the larger Rainbow Ballroom. The Ballroom doubled as an indoor basketball court and was also the site of several Yarmouth town meetings. Not long afterward, an outdoor wrestling arena was built on the site of the old Pavilion featuring some of the better-known grapplers on the east coast. Amateur boxing matches also drew large crowds to the area.

After World War II, the wrestling arena continued to feature matches with such attractions as Gorgeous George versus Elephant Boy and the Mighty Midget. Under promoter Fred Bruno, night contests were held in the circular fenced in arena under the new floodlights. Local boys from Chatham to Falmouth would square off in a preliminary bout to set up the feature marquee performers like Frank Sexton, billed in 1948 as the world's champion of professional wrestlers.

It seems that the wrestling matches were not always on the level. The owner of a nearby restaurant had the concession to sell hot dogs to the fans. Never sure how many he would need to feed, his job was made much easier when the promoter told him when the feature match was going to end. The hot dog supplier always hoped for at least three falls. Longer matches always meant more hot dog sales.

Gradually, the public's appetite shifted away from wrestling matches. The circus still set up there into the 1950's, but by the end of the decade the site was largely vacant. Today, Mill Hill is crowned by a large complex of time-share units. It is doubtful that any of the people who stay at this resort have any idea of what events took place there a half century ago.

Kettle Pond to Coliseum

During a typical Cape Cod winter there are only a handful of weeks in January and February when the cold temperatures can sufficiently freeze the local kettle pond to support a pick up hockey game. Codders of old knew this well, as they took advantage of these chilly days to harvest pond ice.

Up until 1957, any ice-skating on Cape took place on her ponds. Yet, that year, with a $150,000 contribution from the Kennedy family, a skating rink was opened in Hyannis—the Joseph P. Kennedy Memorial Skating Rink, named for JFK's elder brother who was killed in World War II. It opened in November of that year after one year of construction, with its first contest ending in a tie: Barnstable North Side men 14—Barnstable South Side men 14.

In those days the rink consisted of an uncovered ice surface surrounded by boards. Skaters laced up in an adjacent building, called the "warming house," which held the manager's office and a concession stand. Without a roof, the ice was subject to the elements, including snow that needed to be shoveled before a game could be played. It was not until the mid-1960's when a roof was eventually constructed.

Hockey on Cape Cod has a long and storied history, beginning with the Cape Cod Amateur Hockey League formed in the late-1950's. Teams included Barnstable, Yarmouth-Dennis, Falmouth, Plymouth, and Middleboro. Plymouth later left the league and was replaced with a team from Mattapoisett, which was later replaced by a Hyannis team. Throughout the 1960's, league games could attract hundreds of fans, with twice as many attending playoff games.

During the early 1970's, hockey-mania spread throughout the region with the Boston Bruins' two Stanley Cup championships in 1970 and '72. The 46,000-square foot Cape Cod Coliseum was opened in South Yarmouth, with seating for 5,000, so the amateur league made the move to the larger venue. The league disbanded a few years later, though, but that was certainly not the end of hockey on the peninsula. Professional hockey arrived on Cape the same year that the Coliseum opened in the form of the Cape Cod Cubs, part of the Eastern Hockey League. Former Boston Bruin Bronco Horvath coached the team to win the East Hockey League

Central Division title. Yet success was short-lived as the league failed after its second season.

North American Hockey League action came to the Coliseum in 1975 with the Cape Codders hockey team, but by February of the following year the club folded due to financial difficulties. Next came the New England Freedoms in 1979, a team of the North Eastern League, yet their stay on Cape Cod was only a few months. They were followed by the Cape Cod Buccaneers of the Atlantic Coast Hockey League in 1981. Though they were scheduled to play 34 home games at the Coliseum over the course of their season, they folded within three months.

Women also laced up their skates to play hockey on Cape. As part of the South Shore Women's Hockey League, the Cape Cod Aces, founded in 1977, took on all challengers including college teams. They won a number of titles in state and national tournaments.

World Hockey Association (WHA) and National Hockey League (NHL) games were played on Cape Cod. The first WHA game held at the Coliseum took place in 1974 between the New England Whalers and the Quebec Nordiques. Both teams are now in the NHL (the New England Whalers became the Hartford Whalers and are now the Carolina Hurricanes, while the Quebec Nordiques are now the Colorado Avalanche).

As for NHL hockey on Cape, the Boston Bruins played a pre-season exhibition game against the Buffalo Sabres at the Coliseum on October 6, 1979. The Bruins won the contest 5-4, with Terry O'Reilly being credited with the winning goal. It seems that with the game tied and a delayed penalty called on the Bruins, the Sabres pulled their goaltender in favor of an extra man. With the Buffalo goal empty ... and Bruin O'Reilly attacking in the opponent's zone ... a Buffalo defenseman accidentally shot the puck into his own goal!

The Barbarians
Many young Cape Codders have pictured themselves as someday reaching the heights of popular music with a hit recording and a loyal fan following. One local band that actually made it for at least a brief moment in the national spotlight was a Provincetown group known as the "Barbarians." In 1965 they recorded a song that

reached as high as 55 on the Billboard top 100 charts. The tune landed them a contract with Laurie Records and put them on the stage with such big time musical icons as James Brown, the Beach Boys, Marvin Gaye, the Rolling Stones, Chuck Berry, and the Supremes.

Bruce Benson, Geoff Morris, Jerry Causi, and Victor "Moulty" Moulton made up the Barbarians. They were home grown musicians who got their first gig at the Rumpus Room in the back of the Old Colony Tap in the summer of 1964. Moulton was the most interesting member of the band. It was he who gave the group its name and he became its signature performer. What was unique about "Moulty" was that he was the drummer, but he only had one hand. As a youngster he put together a homemade pipe bomb stuffed with about 2,000 match heads. When it exploded prematurely, he lost his left hand. Fitted with an artificial prosthesis that wasn't much more than a hook, he took up the drums. One of his cousins put in a good word for the group to Leonard Enos, who owned the Rumpus Room. The group played there every night during the summer of 1964, getting paid a percentage of how much beer was sold each night. If nothing else, it beat the old gig of diving for quarters off Macmillan Wharf when the Boston boat would arrive in town.

What pushed the Barbarians to national fame was a song they recorded near the end of the year, called "Are You a Boy, Or Are You a Girl?" It was a tune that seemed not only to fit the changing social scene at the Cape tip but also the nascent androgynous leanings of a growing segment of the nation's youth. It was actually a fun song that kids could dance to and it caught the attention of several managers and record companies.

In 1965, the group played at the Teenage International Music Awards in Santa Monica, California where they shared the stage with some of America's greatest pop stars. Their fifteen minutes of fame carried them through the early 1970's when they drifted apart. But their one hit song continues to be a legend in Provincetown and when it is occasionally played on the oldies stations, most "boomers" who grew up on Cape Cod remember with a smile those summer days of innocence and wonder.

Chapter 9

20th Century – From Telephones to Wicked Witches

Now that we are in a new century, the 20th has become part of Cape Cod history. Such events as the arrival of the telephone and the advent of air travel tell of technological advances, while the election of the first woman (Cape Cod born and raised) to the Massachusetts legislature indicates advancement on a different scale.

Telephone Arrives on Cape

History tells us that the telephone emerged from the 19th century experiments of Alexander Graham Bell and David Edward Hughes. Bell's first telephone communication of "Watson, come here, I need you!" dates to 1876.

Soon afterwards, the new technology appeared on Cape Cod when a Professor Robinson arrived in Sandwich to demonstrate the device. A wire was run from the Congregational Church to the town hall where a crowd had gathered to watch and listen. Suddenly, music from the church was heard over a receiver in the town hall. The locals were perplexed. Some considered it a trick. Despite the crowd's sense of awe, Professor Robinson left town without making a single sale.

Cape Cod was late getting telephone service compared to other places in Massachusetts, perhaps due to its rural environment, its distance from a major city, and its lower than average economic base. Service did arrive locally during the 1880's with lines linking the Cape to the telephone system of New Bedford. With that, Cape Cod became connected to the rest of Massachusetts and the country.

An 1886 directory was published for Southeastern Massachusetts Telephone Company of New Bedford. One of the first in Dennis to own a telephone was Luther Hall, who had a line connecting his home to his nearby store. But as his was the only one in town he could communicate with no one else. Among Yarmouth's first telephone owners were Dr. Thomas Pulsifer and T.T. Hallet's drug store. The telephone switchboard at Hyannis was in place by the early 1890s. In those days the caller cranked his or her phone to reach an operator at "central" and then asked to be connected with the party being called.

Just after the turn of the century Sandwich had less than ten telephones, while Falmouth had about sixty subscribers. Special offers helped increase the Falmouth subscribership to over two hundred by 1907. Telephone poles were erected in a number of Cape Cod towns, and miles of telephone lines connected communities. By 1910, Harwich and the southern villages of Dennis had more than two hundred telephone owners. As more people obtained telephones the number of switchboards increased and the switchboards themselves were enlarged to handle all the connections. This technology would forever change small town life, with Cape Cod shaking off the dust of her earlier century and stepping boldly into the new age.

Earliest Born Actor in Motion Pictures

Bourne summer resident Joseph Jefferson, who owned a home on Buttermilk Bay, was America's premier 19th century comic actor and a singular stage personality who helped to define the art form. He spent many happy times with family and friends at his Cape manor house—dubbed the "Crow's Nest." In fact, one of those friends was President Grover Cleveland, who kept a summer place at nearby Monument Beach. Together they would hunt and fish throughout the region, including at Wakeby Pond in Mashpee where today two islands in the pond bear their names.

Born in Philadelphia in 1829, Jefferson's lineage included a number of stage performers, including his father (an actor and manager), his mother (a singer), and his paternal grandfather and great-grandfather (both actors). Jefferson began acting at three years old when he performed in *Pizarro*. As he grew older he became a stock actor, traveling from city to city to perform. In 1859, he got his big break when he appeared in more than 150 performances of

Our American Cousin. Later he performed in *Nickolas Nickleby* and *The Rivals.*

While in England during 1865 he played Rip Van Winkle, a role with which he would be linked for the rest of his career. He played the Washington Irving character to perfection over the next four decades, both on stage and in motion pictures. In fact, Jefferson appeared in a handful of silent movies between 1896 and 1903, in each picture playing his famous Rip Van Winkle character. Motion pictures were first introduced near the end of 1895, and because Jefferson was in his late-60's when he appeared on film in 1896, he is generally considered to be the earliest born motion picture actor.

There is a footnote to this story. According to Josef Berger, author of the book *Cape Cod Pilot*, "Jefferson wanted to buy a house in Sandwich, but Sandwich didn't want Jefferson. To the townsfolk, 'the stage' was a remote, godless world, whence no good neighbor could have come. Jefferson went south, but before he left, he bought a lot in Bay View Cemetery, and told his friends, 'They won't let me live in Sandwich, but I'll stay there yet!'"

Actor Joe Jefferson and his home on Buttermilk Bay. (Jim Coogan collection)

In death, Jefferson got the last laugh, for he was buried in
Sandwich. His grave is marked by a large boulder adorned with a
bas-relief image of his profile. The other side has a plaque displaying the words "And yet we are but tenants, let us assure ourselves
of this, and then it will not be so hard to make room for the new
administration, for shortly the great landlord will give us notice
that our lease has expired."

Long rest Joseph Jefferson, 1829—1905.

Bridge Out

On January 25, 1905, a winter storm visited Cape Cod. Winds and
tides pushed water and ice up Bass River, and flooded into Grand
Cove. There the liquid mass slammed into a wooden bridge which
spanned the entrance of the cove and connected the communities
of West Dennis and South Dennis.

Since 1854, the bridge formed a shortcut for travelers from the
southern village of West Dennis to the train depot located at South
Dennis. As well, youngsters used the bridge to make their way to
school in the next village. Locals made use of the bridge to transport
goods to the train for shipment to buyers. Yet, Mother Nature
understood none of this, and in the end the extreme nature of the
winter storm and her powerful surge severed the wooden connection. Cove Road was suddenly cut in two.

Immediately, there were cries to rebuild the bridge. At the same
time, another faction formed to keep the connection severed and
the communities separated. The bridge became an issue that divided the town, opening old wounds of a north versus south struggle
that had almost seen the town divided into two during the previous
century. An article was added to the town meeting of that February
"to see if the town will vote to discontinue Grand Cove bridge, so
called." When the votes were counted, it was decided to indeed
"discontinue the bridge." Travelers between the two villages were
forced to go around the cove, adding nearly a mile to the journey.

An article later appeared in the March 4 issue of the *Yarmouth
Register* newspaper, asking residents to reconsider the bridge issue.
Here are some excerpts:

"At the town meeting recently held, it was voted to abolish the
Cove bridge … Thus a large number of people are deprived of a

great convenience in what seems to have been in a very offhand manner ... The bridge furnished a short cut between the south and west portions of the town and to points beyond. We vote to build macadam roads for those who wish to speed their trotters and automobiles ... Is it too much to ask that a few dollars also be used to keep in repair a bridge which accommodates many hundreds a year of those, who still depend on foot power for locomotion?"

Opponents claimed that "an average of one person a day" used the bridge while those from West Dennis countered that those in the northern villages were misinformed. A further article appeared in the March 11 issue mentioning a petition circulating in West Dennis. Nearly one hundred "friends of the bridge" signed the petition. According to the article, "The prime movers in this matter are well-known business men, who recognize the fact that the absence of the bridge is a serious detriment to business in this section of the town, and that to abolish it will cause the property situated on this thoroughfare to depreciate in value."

"As the town is, or should be, one united family, and what is for the good of one is for the benefit of all, we trust that this appeal will meet with a response from all who have at heart a sincere regard for the welfare of the people."

At an April meeting, county commissioners "decided that it could not be abolished, but must be rebuilt." Still, no progress was made on the issue of rebuilding the bridge, prompting another article to appear in the *Yarmouth Register* on January 27, 1906, just after the one-year anniversary of the bridge's demise. "It is to be hoped that the friends of the Cove bridge will take steps toward its rebuilding in the coming town meeting. It is a serious inconvenience to many people of the town to have it in its present condition."

Further appeals over subsequent years met with no positive results. One hundred years later the bridge remains "out" as the opposite ends of Cove Road—one end at West Dennis and the other end at South Dennis—stare at each other across the water.

Starling Burgess: Architect of Air and Sea
One of America's pioneer aviators had a strong Cape Cod connection. W. Starling Burgess was the son of Sandwich-born Edward Burgess,

who was a nationally known naval architect and designer of several 19th century America's Cup yachts. Starling Burgess followed in his father's footsteps.

In 1905, at the age of 27, and after naval service as a gunner's mate in the Spanish American War, he opened a yacht yard in Marblehead, Massachusetts. At the same time that he was designing and building yachts, he became interested in aviation. He signed up as one of the first students of the Wright Company and designed and built the first airplane to fly in New England, an event that happened in 1910. In 1911, he fitted a biplane with pontoons and was the first pilot to take off from and land on water.

During this early phase of aviation, Burgess could occasionally be seen flying around Cape Cod, no doubt stopping to visit his extended family in the Bourne and Sandwich areas. A witness to one of those early flights recalled the wonder of it all.

"It was 1912. While I was on my way to the Cataumet railroad station, a small truck was coming. Something queer was attached to the back of it. It pulled up beside the road and stopped. I went over to look at it. 'Why it was a flying machine!' The first on Cape Cod. Starling Burgess and a helper were making adjustments. Soon they started off down the road. I followed behind. They unloaded

Starling Burgess and the first airplane to land on Cape Cod. (Bourne Town Archives)

the machine on Scraggy Neck causeway near the water. After awhile, Mr. Burgess slowed up after making a few more adjustments. He got in. He asked my uncle if he wanted to go up but auntie said, 'No!' He went downwind, turned and started coming towards me. He was going at a terrific speed. Slowly he arose above the water and began circling overhead. Everyone was stretching their necks. A man in the air!"

Burgess's fascination with aviation won him the Collier trophy in 1913 for the greatest achievement in aviation during the previous year—the design of a self-stabilizing airplane. The Wright Brothers and the legendary Glenn Curtis had won the prize before him. When World War I began, Burgess delivered the first American-built airplane to the allies. Just before America's involvement in the war, he merged his interest with the Curtis Aeroplane Company and built seaplanes and blimps for the Navy. At the war's end, Burgess took some time off, cruising the Caribbean islands for a couple of years. Later, he landed in Provincetown where he lived for almost a decade, shuttling between the Cape tip and the north shore where his yacht business was located. One of his draftsmen in these years was the later-to-be-famous, L. Francis Herreshoff.

During this period, Burgess re-connected with naval architecture, the subject that had marked his father's fame. He designed and built yachts for wealthy clients including Charles Francis Adams and Harold Vanderbilt. He laid out the aluminum sparred *Enterprise,* which won the 1930 America's Cup race against the British yacht *Shamrock V.* In 1934, his *Rainbow* defeated British challenger *Endeavor.* Just three years later, working with naval architect Olin Stephens, he designed the J-class *Ranger,* which defended the Cup against a very outclassed *Endeavor II,* and defeated the British yacht in four straight victories. Later he pioneered the twelve-meter yachts that are now standard in the America's Cup races. During World War II Burgess was employed as a civilian engineer for the Navy.

As vigorous in his married life as he was as a designer—he had five wives—Starling Burgess died in March of 1947. One of the legacies of these relationships was his daughter, Tasha Tudor, a well known illustrator of children's books in America.

Two Constables and a Quart

During the 1920's, Cape Cod, like much of the rest of the country, winked at Prohibition. Locals could make a quick dollar in the rum running business and people who asked were often directed to a nearby roadhouse or "speak easy" where some "ardent spirits" could be obtained.

Still, the law that prohibited the sale of alcohol was on the books and, occasionally, it was even enforced. Perhaps the most unusual case of this type that came up on Cape Cod happened in 1924 when one of Harwich's three law enforcement officials attempted to arrest one of his brother officers on the charge of selling illegal liquor in the town.

It all started at Emulous E. Hall's barn in North Harwich. A Hyannis man named Coughlin was in town looking for a drink and he met up with local resident Homer Martin. Martin told Coughlin that he knew where he could buy some liquor and he proceeded to take the Hyannis man over to the home of Emulous Hall. Hall ran a grocery store at the North Harwich depot. He was also one of the three constables in the town. These were the days before there was any real police force in Harwich and constables were elected with powers like those of a deputy sheriff. They were charged with keeping the peace and seeing that the laws of the Commonwealth were enforced.

When the two men arrived at Hall's house, Martin told Hall that his friend was interested in buying some liquor. Hall went out behind his barn and came back with a quart of bonded whiskey. What neither Hall nor Martin knew was that Coughlin had been hired as a spotter to ferret out illegal liquor sales in the town by Constable Roger Bassett, another Harwich law officer. Later, Coughlin reported to Bassett and told him that he had purchased the quart from Hall and that Martin had served as an agent. Bassett then swore out a warrant against his fellow officer and also Martin for complicity in the illegal sale of liquor.

By the time the case came before the Second District Court, there was great interest across the Cape. No one could remember when one law official had hauled another before the bar of justice. Coughlin recounted the events from the time he contacted Martin until the jug was on the front seat of his car. Bassett, in his testimony, went further and said that it was clear to him that Hall had knowingly violated the law because he had the liquor hidden out of sight behind the barn. "I asked him on a number of occasions if he had any liquor on his property and he always denied it," said Bassett. "I later went and verified that the liquor was hidden there." It seemed to be an open and shut case.

Homer Martin took the stand in his own defense and stated that when the quart was handed into the car by Hall there had been no request for a payment. Martin told Judge Heman A. Harding that the quart was a gift for a previous favor that Hall owed him. Under cross-examination, Coughlin admitted that when he asked, Martin had indeed told him that there was no charge for the liquor. But Coughlin insisted that he had given Martin eight dollars for it. "Did you put it in his hand? asked the judge. "Not exactly, " said Coughlin. "I left it on the seat when I got out of the car." Martin claimed he never saw the money until hours later when he was putting his car away for the night.

When Emulous Hall was called to testify he told the court that he had been to Boston the week previous and had come home with some liquor for himself and for his friend Martin. When he arrived at his house, which he shared with his sister, there was company and not wanting to embarrass her he hid the liquor behind the barn, intending to bring it in later. He said that Martin had done favors for him in the past and when Martin asked for some liquor for his friend, he had intended it as payment for those favors. "I never expected to be paid money for it, Judge," he stated.

Since it was not illegal to possess liquor and it appeared that no sale had been intended, Judge Harding had little choice but to rule that there was no case. A simple gift of liquor to a friend was not a crime. Constable Hall was found not guilty.

When Captain Dan Had A Plan

Sometimes the government does strange things. And probably no action sparked more head scratching and Monday morning quarterbacking than in 1925 when the Navy Department made the decision to risk a valuable submarine in transit by refusing to use the Cape Cod Canal. And it all revolved around the attempt to avoid spending $156.80.

It was a cold winter day in mid-January when the submarine *S-19* slipped out of Boston Harbor bound for New London, Connecticut. The 220-foot long undersea boat carried a crew of 34 men and four officers. It would have seemed natural that the ship should have plotted a course from Boston down through the Cape Cod Canal, Buzzards Bay, and then on to Connecticut Sound, rather than risk a passage around the Cape. But this was 1925 and the Canal was in private ownership and the ship's captain was under orders to avoid paying unnecessary expenses. The Navy Department had decided that the $136.80 fee for Canal passage, plus $20.00 for a pilot, was too much for the budget. The captain was told to take the long way around. Unlike modern submarines that travel submerged 95% of the time, the *S-19*, which had been laid down just after World War I, was really a surface craft that submerged only when making an approach for a torpedo attack. On the surface in heavy weather, however, she was not a good sea boat.

In the early morning hours of January 14, off course and buffeted by heavy seas, the *S-19* fetched up near the entrance of Nauset Harbor. Even with a high sea running, the surfmen at the Nauset Coast Guard Station, under the command of Captain Abbot Walker, launched a boat into the gray dawn to try to get a line on the stricken vessel. Observers watched in horror when a roller caught the small boat and upended it. The six men were thrown into the sea and only through some sort of miracle were they able to cling to the sides of the overturned boat and regain the safety of land. No further attempts to get near the submarine took place until later in the afternoon when a Coast Guard cutter from Woods Hole arrived on the scene. Still, it was another day and a half before the submarine crew were taken off the vessel, which now lay hard aground about 100 yards off shore.

Attempts to refloat the submarine commenced immediately. The Navy brought in engineers and experts who proposed several plans to move the submarine off its sandy perch. Tugboats carrying heavy duty hawsers were brought down from the Charlestown Navy Yard and they attempted to pull the *S-19* off the bar by brute force. But the east wind, coupled with a constant surf at the mouth of the harbor, defeated their efforts. Weeks went by and the submarine stayed right where she was.

About this time, someone called the authorities' attention to an Orleans man named Dan Gould. Captain Gould had been a packet master on the old *Nettie M. Rogers,* running between Orleans and Providence, Rhode Island. Now retired, he was a general jack-of-all-trades—particularly when it came to matters related to the sea.

Submarine S-19 ashore at Nauset Harbor, January 1925. (Stan Snow Collection)

When he was brought in to the temporary office of the Naval engineers, Captain Gould was asked if he thought the tugs could be successful in pulling the submarine out to deep water. "Nope," was his reply. If they added more line and perhaps another tug, would it work then? "Nope," came the same answer. The officials were getting a bit annoyed at what they perceived was a seemingly impertinent local man. Well, what if we dredge a channel out to deep water? How about that? They looked at Captain Gould. "Nope, too much cross channel currents out there," the Cape man elaborated.

The officials looked at each other and finally asked Captain Gould if he had a better plan. "Yep," he answered and he proceeded to draw a simple sketch showing a heavy anchor planted solidly about 200 yards out from the stranded sub and a cable hooked from the vessel through an eight fall block on the buoyed anchor, then back to shore, where the line would be attached to a small steam engine. "When the tide is high," explained Gould, "Start the engine and the rising sea, coupled with the leverage from the block, should pull her off nicely."

Probably figuring that the Orleans man was mocking their efforts because he made it seem so simple, the officials filed the plan and went back to trying to pull the S-19 out to sea with the tugboats. After another week of futility, they decided to give Captain Gould's idea a try. Once in place, the cable was hooked to a reel and, as the tide came in, the steam engine took a strain on the line and the submarine started heading out stern first, to deeper water. As she floated free, a tug swung in close and put a line on the S-19.

Captain Gould never got so much as a thank you from the Navy. He later told friends that they didn't even offer to pay for his ticket on the train back to Orleans. Several months later a Congressional investigation headed by Charles L. Gifford castigated the Navy for spending thousands of dollars in salvage money to refloat the S-19. Captain Gould's efforts in the matter were never mentioned. Officials seemed more embarrassed by the fact that a two million dollar submarine had been put in harm's way, all because the Navy wanted to save $156.80.

A Woman in the House

Cape Cod has produced a number of important women. Mercy Otis Warren of West Barnstable was a political satirist during the Revolutionary War. Katharine Lee Bates of Falmouth penned "America the Beautiful." Both have been immortalized with monuments located in their respective home towns.

A 20th century Cape woman who rose to prominence was Sylvia Donaldson of Falmouth. In 1923, she was sworn in as a Republican member of the Massachusetts House of Representatives and became the first woman legislator in the history of the State. Only three years earlier, the Nineteenth Amendment granted women the vote after a long suffrage battle about which Donaldson once wrote: "All people cannot vote—women, minors and lunatics are prohibited."

Born Mersivia Donaldson on July 12, 1849, to parents George W. and Betsey Ann Donaldson, she spent her first 24 years in Falmouth. After receiving a degree from Boston University, she returned to teach in Falmouth for a time. (One of her pupils was Katharine Lee Bates.) She later left Falmouth to teach in Brockton for more than four decades before becoming a principal in the Brockton School District.

Besides serving on the Massachusetts School Board, she was also involved in the National Education Association, the League of Women Voters, the Audubon Society, the Women's Civic Federation, the Daughters of the American Revolution, the Women's Republican Club of Boston (which she helped form), the Plymouth County Teacher's Association (where she served as president), the Junior Red Cross (as chairperson), and the Brockton Public Library (as trustee). And she was at Camp Devens during World War I, where some 100,000 soldiers were processed prior to deployment to Europe. Public service was her life.

After her retirement, at the age of 70, Donaldson made Massachusetts history by winning election to the House of Representatives from Brockton. Her tenure saw Prohibition, the transatlantic flight of Charles Lindbergh, the Sacco and Vanzetti case, and the Stock Market Crash of 1929. She won reelection three times, fighting for issues of concern to women, children, and education. In recognition of "her splendid service," on February 18,

1926 she served briefly as Speaker of the House during a session that saw legislators consider a bill that would declare it mandatory for women to serve on juries. The Madam Speaker opposed the bill, feeling it would be a hardship for mothers. Her impassioned speech against the legislation aided in its defeat.

Though Donaldson left political office in 1930 at the age of 80, she continued to be involved in Brockton education through 1933. She remained in contact with many of her former students throughout her life, and there is evidence of her connection with the family of Katharine Lee Bates as late as September 1930 in the form of a letter to the poet's brother, Arthur Lee Bates of Portland, Maine.

After fracturing her hip in a fall at her Brockton apartment, Donaldson's health deteriorated. She died on June 15, 1937 and was buried at Falmouth's Oak Grove Cemetery.

The Largest Indoor Canvas Mural in the World
The Cape Cinema building in Dennis is well known for the huge canvas that covers the ceiling. It is a representation of the heavens done in an art deco style that was popular in the 1930's when it was painted. With shades of blue, gold, and orange, the mural features

The Cape Cinema. (Jack Sheedy photo)

a surrealistic universe juxtaposing celestial and human bodies. At 6,400 square feet, and stretching arch-like over the cinema seats, it is the largest single indoor canvas in the world. Yet, what is not generally known about the magnificent work is that the artist, Rockwell Kent, saw it only once in place although he lived for more than 30 years after he finished it.

When Raymond Moore was looking to cap the interior design of his new cinema building he chose Rockwell Kent, an illustrator of stark and rugged landscapes, to do the ceiling mural. The choice of Kent was controversial. He was a political maverick and a self-avowed socialist. The artist was a man who held strong political opinions and who defied convention in his pursuit of nonconformity. Kent's paintings reflected his adventurous life, much of which had been spent in the solitude of extreme latitudes. Before he was thirty years old he had sailed to Cape Horn, and lived in Greenland, Newfoundland, and Alaska. His paintings and lithographs took on the distinctive flavor of the austere landscapes that he explored—rugged mountains, haunting sea, and barren wilderness.

Kent put together the Cape Cinema painting in sections at his 200-acre farm and studio near Ausable Forks, New York. His assistant was Ellen Goldsborough. At its completion, the separate pieces of the mural were put on railroad cars and shipped to Dennis where, under the direction of noted Broadway set designer Jo Mielziner, it was installed. Kent had told Moore he wanted nothing to do with the final hanging of the mural because he had a quarrel with Massachusetts. When the alleged anarchists Nicola Sacco and Bartolomeo Vanzetti were tried and executed by the Commonwealth in 1927, Kent believed that the two men had been murdered by Massachusetts. He vowed that he would never visit the state again.

As the June 1930 dedication date approached, Kent's lingering anger at Massachusetts threatened to keep him away from unveiling perhaps his greatest work. Only because Moore begged him to see the mural in place did Kent break his vow to never again enter Massachusetts. He arrived one day in late June and stayed just long enough to sign the mural. He refused to accept the commission on it and gave the money to a friend. Then he left town and so far as anyone knows, he never set foot in Massachusetts again.

Wicked Witch of Dennis

Dennis boasts a number of "firsts." During the 18th century, East Dennis' "Sleepy" John Sears, a sea captain by trade, was the first American to develop a workable method of harvesting salt from the sea through solar evaporation. Henry Hall conducted experiments on his Dennis farm to determine the best conditions in which to grow cranberries, thus forming the beginnings of a cranberry industry that still flourishes today.

In the 20th century, Dennis' Cape Playhouse was known as a stage where some of the country's greatest actors—notably Henry Fonda and Bette Davis—first got their start. And on those same grounds, the town of Dennis may have had another "first."

During 1939, the Cape Cinema located next to the Playhouse was chosen as one of just a handful of cinemas around the country to serve as the premiere for the film, *The Wizard of Oz*. In fact, a Playhouse playbill from that period advertised the film's Dennis premiere on August 11. Other sources point to the official world premiere as occurring on August 12 at the Strand Theatre in Oconomowoc, Wisconsin. This was followed by the Hollywood premiere at Grauman's Chinese Theatre on August 15. Yet, the Dennis premiere appears to predate the Wisconsin showing. Does this prove that the Cape Cinema in Dennis, Massachusetts was the venue for the very first public showing of the classic film?

In the Playhouse playbill the film was promoted as "Hollywood's most famous and original screen musical" and as "MGM's musical comedy triumph in color!" The article goes on to praise the film's actors, which included Margaret Hamilton, claiming that she "is perfect as the Wicked Witch."

Incidentally, the town of Dennis played another first—this time in the career of the actress who played the Wicked Witch of the West. It seems that Miss Hamilton, who besides her witch role is also remembered for her appearances in Maxwell House coffee television commercials during the 1970's, made her acting debut in 1930 at ... you guessed it ... the Cape Playhouse.

Chapter 10

20th Century – From Brando to Hurricane Bob

The second half of the 20th century saw the arrival of a number of hurricanes, the JFK presidency, a couple of WWII German spies, and nearly the United Nations. We conclude here with some more recent tales to round out the century that was.

Hurricane of '44

The Great Atlantic Hurricane of 1944, as it was known in the days before hurricanes were named, visited this peninsula on the evening and early morning of September 14 and 15 of that year. The high winds and tides were felt throughout the Cape, bringing down buildings, destroying coastal businesses, eroding beaches, and even sinking *Vineyard Lightship* #73 along with her twelve-man crew. Stationed off Cuttyhunk Island, the vessel would not be found until nearly 20 years later when her battered hull was located on the bottom in more than 100 feet of water just south of New Bedford. Off the coast five Naval vessels were also sunk with the loss of over 350 lives.

The storm track initially hit Cape Hatteras a day earlier and continued to move up the coast in a northeasterly trajectory. Further landfalls were made at Long Island, New York and at the Connecticut/Rhode Island border before its path took it east through Massachusetts. The hurricane finally played itself out along the coast of Maine.

In contrast to the Hurricane of 1938, which took locals completely by surprise (killing 15 on Cape Cod, washing away over four miles of railroad tracks at Falmouth, and destroying the drawbridge at Woods Hole, among other damage), Cape Codders received warnings of the 1944 storm via reports aired on WOCB—the Cape's only radio station at the time. Reports though, ended abruptly in the early evening when the station's broadcasting tower in West Yarmouth was downed by winds. At just after midnight, a barometer reading of 28.85 was recorded at Squaw Island near Hyannis Port. As the winds peaked at over 100 miles an hour, a Chatham doctor said that the sharp wind was "like the teeth of a rake." Another observer said that the sky looked almost like the sea with its fast moving rolling and billowing clouds.

Centuries old trees came down along the Cape's north side. The south coast was hit particularly hard. The beautiful silver leaf poplars that had shaded West Dennis and South Yarmouth were overturned. Houses and businesses were washed away and the ten foot tidal surge pushed boats a mile inland from Nantucket Sound. The surge also contaminated wells in much of the Cape. Bridges were out at Herring River, Swan River, and Parkers River and Libby's Chowder House restaurant in South Yarmouth ended up on the other side of Route 28 from its normal location.

Churches suffered great damage. At West Dennis, the spire of the Methodist Church was toppled and driven like a huge spike through the roof of the building. The Congregational Church in Yarmouth Port also lost its steeple. Also damaged was the old Indian Church in Mashpee. The side walls of the First Universalist Church in Chatham were ripped away.

At Camp Edwards, a major training center for the war effort, the roof of the mess hall was completely blown off and storage buildings were littered around the base. German prisoners of war, housed at the base, were enlisted in helping with the clean up. In February of 1945, a number of portable saw mills were brought to the Cape and the prisoners cut thousands of board feet of downed lumber.

Later, the storms of the 1950's were given names. But for people who lived through the Hurricane of 1944, the storm had already delivered its personal calling card as nature's wartime killer.

The Spies Who Loved Music
Just like those urban myths—alligators in the Boston sewers, etc.—Cape Cod has its own mythology. Many stories, no doubt originating in the imaginations or perhaps the clouded experience

of someone's mind, can make us wonder. Usually there is just enough truth in the circumstances surrounding the tale that we can't just dismiss it out of hand. One such story recently came from a lower Cape nursing home. And while it cannot be proved, it still gives us pause. Could it have happened?

A man whose business was repairing coin operated juke boxes got a call to service some machines on the outer Cape. It was during World War II and it was difficult to get gasoline. After some serious horse trading with friends, he finally got enough to make the trip. He suggested that his wife come with him and they would make it into a working vacation. The couple took a cottage near Cahoon's Hollow in Wellfleet. The man would pick up machines that needed attention and set them out in the living room of the cottage where he could work on them. As he tinkered, his wife enjoyed the sun outside.

One evening the couple decided to go out for dinner. Even though it was August, the Cape was quiet. The war had pretty much dried up the tourist business and the atmosphere was more like September than summer. There were few restaurants open and they had to drive back to Orleans to find one. After eating, the two started to drive back to Wellfleet in a heavy fog. With the headlights reduced to mere slits because of the blackout, they could barely see the road ahead. There was actually little danger because it seemed that no one was on the road but them. Not being familiar with the area, the man turned where he thought the cottage was and found himself on a narrow sandy track that seemed to go nowhere. Suddenly, out of the fog two men jumped in front of the car. They were armed coastguardsmen and they demanded that the couple explain what they were doing in this remote area.

"We're lost," said the man. "We thought we were near our cottage but we took the wrong road in the fog."

"This is a restricted area after dark," said one of the guardsmen. "We have a report that German spies may have come ashore from a submarine and we've increased patrols all along the beach. You had better turn around and get out of here right now."

After getting directions from the guardsmen, the couple turned their car around and eventually found the right road to their cottage. When they arrived, it was almost midnight.

"That was some story," said the man. "I doubt there is a German within a thousand miles of this beach.

His wife nodded and entered the cottage. On the table in the living room was a juke box that the man had just finished repairing. As the couple started to get ready for bed, the machine suddenly started to play a song. Moving to it, the man examined it closely. In the coin box there were three coins—all German. The last one had apparently been stuck in the slot mechanism and had fallen into the machine when the door to the cottage had slammed shut in the wind.

Cape Cod and the United Nations

Imagine an angry Nikita Kruschev banging his shoe at the United Nations General Assembly building—on Cape Cod. How about the appearances of Fidel Castro or Nelson Mandela at the internationally recognized Cape Cod headquarters of the world body. It all might have been part of Cape Cod's history if, right after World War II, the United Nations preparatory commission had chosen Camp Edwards and its 25,000 surrounding acres as the site for the new headquarters for the organization instead of New York City.

In the fall of 1945, as the world celebrated the end of the war, the question arose as to where a permanent location for the United Nations might be. There was much lobbying by European nations to put it there, but war damage limited many of the options on that continent. Emerging as the leader of the free world, the United States also wanted the prestige of being the new home of the United Nations. A twelve-nation subcommittee was put together to choose six possible locations along the east coast. It was felt that a place somewhere between Boston and New York would be most suitable. Almost like today's bids for the Olympic games, a number of localities submitted proposals. Among these were New Haven, Connecticut; Newport, Rhode Island; Bar Harbor, Maine; and Concord and Lexington in Massachusetts.

On Cape Cod, William Peters, the president of the Falmouth Board of Trade, saw a golden opportunity to grab the U.N. headquarters for this area. "Cape Cod has just what the United Nations Organization says it wants," Mr. Peters noted. "We offer the nearest continental location to Europe. We are nearest by 150 miles to

South America. Travel to the United Nations Organization headquarters will be by air. In Otis Field we have the finest airport
in New England. We have the finest climate in the East—cool in the
summer and mild in the winter. We are right between Boston and
New York. We have the room which the United Nations
Organization will need for expansion of its headquarters."

While there was initial skepticism about such a plan for Cape
Cod, others saw merit in the argument. Donald Trayser, who was
president of the Cape Cod Chamber of Commerce, sent a cable
to the site committee in London asking that body to consider
Cape Cod as the location for the U.N. headquarters. The cable
was endorsed by Charles Megathlin, chairman of the Barnstable
County Commissioners. Trayser argued that improved rail
transportation over the already existing route into Camp
Edwards would put Cape Cod just a short ride from Boston. He
also added that, "This peninsula, extending out into the Atlantic
Ocean from southern New England, offers a climate tempered
by the ocean, warmer in winter and cooler in summer, than
the mainland. It [Camp Edwards] offers a wooded land area of
twenty-five thousand acres. Altogether, Cape Cod seems to us
to meet the qualifications for the seat of the United Nations
Organization. We earnestly request that your sub-committee
consider it and if you inspect contemplated sites we urge you to
visit Cape Cod."

Of course, it never happened. With an offer of a free site
along the East River in New York, the subcommittee found itself
with all of the requirements that it had been looking for from
the outset. The decision to place the U.N. headquarters in New
York was made on December 14, 1946. The group never visited
the Cape and the large military reservation that might have
hosted the international organization. And Kruschev, Castro, and
Mandela had to be content with making history in New York and
not Cape Cod.

Brando and Provincetown

In the summer of 1947, author and playwright Tennessee Williams
was spending some vacation time in Provincetown. His new play,
A Streetcar Named Desire, was in the casting stage and director Elia

Kazan called from New York to tell Williams that he was sending a young Greenwich Village actor to the Cape-tip to do an informal reading for the part of Stanley Kowalski.

Marlon Brando was a 24-year old bit player in a few mostly for-gettable off-Broadway productions. He had worked briefly with Kazan in a play called *Trunkline* and had impressed the director with a stage presence charged with sexual energy. Kazan gave the young actor twenty dollars and told him to take a bus to Provincetown to audition for Williams.

Three days later, Kazan called Williams for his reaction to Brando's reading. Williams told him that Brando had not yet arrived. Kazan suspected that Brando was anxious about the audition. He didn't usually do well in them. Brando was not terribly ambitious and preferred life in the bohemian sections of New York where he was comfortable and accepted. Provincetown would have seemed like another world to him. The young actor also wasn't one to surrender to authority and was notorious for not adhering to time schedules. Kazan asked his friend to be patient and to call when Brando arrived.

Brando showed up a couple of days later after hitchhiking to the Cape with a girlfriend. He walked in on Williams dressed in blue jeans and a T-shirt and proceeded to fix a clogged toilet that had plagued the playwright for much of the week. As Williams later wrote to his agent, Audrey Wood, "I had a violent quarrel with the plumber over the phone, so he would not come out. Also the electric wiring broke down and 'plunged us into everlasting darkness' like the Wingfields at supper. All this at once! Oh, and the kitchen was flooded! Marlon arrived in the middle of this domestic cataclysm and set everything straight." Williams added, "He was about the best looking young man that I had ever seen with one or two exceptions!"

To Williams, the actor even looked like Kowalski and when Brando read for the part, Williams was ecstatic. His reading brought an extraordinary strength to the part. Brando was hired on the spot and signed for $550 a week—a huge sum for a young actor who, up until that point, had never had enough money to rent an apartment of his own. The career of one of America's great actors was launched in the shadow of the Pilgrim Monument—a place that may very well have reminded Brando of his beloved Greenwich Village.

I'm Happy Right Here!

Many writers have tried to capture the simple wisdom of Cape Codders. Joe Lincoln, in his Cape-based novels, probably did it as well as anyone. The laconic delivery and common sense logic of the unsophisticated people who hailed from Cape Cod usually trumped the often high-toned and inflated schemes of visitors who always seemed to believe that they had a better way of doing things.

In the early 1950's, commercial aviation was just starting to make inroads among the traveling public. Hyannis airport was bustling with flight service to New York, Boston, and beyond. But not all Cape Codders accepted the new mode of transportation willingly. One local man swore that he'd never fly in an airplane, no matter what the circumstance. "If God wanted us to fly," he reasoned, "Then He'd have given us wings." Interestingly, his wife was very progressive about air travel. She started flying as soon as routes opened up and would regularly soar off to Detroit each year to visit her sister. She could never convince her husband to go with her.

One year she did get him to agree to go out and see his sister-in-law, but he said he'd only go if they took the train. She wasn't happy about it, but she agreed to the condition. Their son drove the pair to Boston where they boarded the train at South Station for the overnight trip to the motor city. A few hours out of Boston, out toward Pittsfield, the train engine started making noises and finally went dead. A yard engine pushed the passenger cars to a siding near an old factory where repairs could be made.

Several boring hours went by and the man's wife became increasingly agitated. As for him, he smoked and read the paper. At one point, the wife stood up and pointed toward the front of the train. "See," she told her husband, "If we had done as I had wanted and flown in an airplane, we'd be there by now."

Calmly the man looked up from his newspaper. "Yes, my dear. That may be true. Engine trouble can be a real nuisance, that's for sure. But if we'd been on the plane of yours and the engine quit, where would we be now? Certainly not in Detroit. I think I'm just as happy being right here on the ground."

His wife sat down and buried her nose in a magazine. And that ended any discussion about how slow the train was.

"Old Shaky"

Throughout the Cold War era the threat of Soviet attack created an ever-present paranoia and dictated US military operations. Air defense systems protected our borders as US planes rigged with radar scanned for Soviet bombers, thus providing the eyes and ears to what might easily culminate in World War III.

As part of our system of defense, an idea was proposed to erect a series of radar platforms some one hundred miles off the United States' east coast to detect an enemy attack. Each structure would resemble an offshore oil platform, such as the ones in the Gulf of Mexico off Texas, thus lending the defense platforms their name. So plans were drawn up to construct five "Texas Towers"—off Portsmouth, NH; south of Yarmouth, Nova Scotia; east of Cape Cod; southeast of Nantucket; and off New York City. They would provide enough warning to scramble interceptor fighters out of Otis Air Base.

The five Texas Towers were designated by number, from TT1 to TT5. Though TT1 off Portsmouth and TT5 off Nova Scotia were never constructed, work began in 1955 on TT2 off Cape Cod. Its 19,000 square-foot triangular platform was built at Quincy, Massachusetts and towed to its position about 110 miles off Chatham. There it was propped atop three gigantic legs in 50 feet of water. Each concrete leg was 12 feet in diameter and over 150 feet in length—50 feet of which rested above water and 50 feet imbedded in the ocean floor.

The following year TT3 rose off Nantucket in 80 feet of water, and in 1957 TT4 was in place southeast of New York in more than 180 feet of water, requiring much longer legs with special braces to provide added support. Yet, not long after becoming operational, the towers proved problematic with an inadequate communications system and a loud rotating radar system that caused the superstructures to vibrate. Add pounding waves and strong winds and it created an inhospitable work environment for the 70-man crew. In fact, TT4 was nicknamed "Old Shaky" because it was known to sway back and forth with the ocean swells.

A number of times fierce weather forced crews to abandon the stations, leaving only a skeleton crew to ride out the storm. Of course, atop a teetering tripod, the men knew that the station beneath their feet was only as stable as its weakest leg. Their predicament was simple: they were alone at sea ... at the mercy of Poseidon.

On January 15, 1961 disaster struck. A number of ocean storms, including Hurricane Donna, battered TT4 and her long, shaky legs. Bracing for yet another storm, the station was left with a 28-man skeleton crew including 14 airmen and 14 civilian repairmen. Hurricane force winds put additional strain on the legs and it's believed a brace gave way. With the aircraft carrier *USS Wasp* making its way toward the swaying tower, TT4 issued a mayday and then, at 7:28 p.m., disappeared from radar. Her long legs had buckled and her platform sank to the ocean's bottom with all hands.

In addition to the 28 lost on TT4, four others were lost to accidents on the other two towers. Further storms continued to lash at TT2 and TT3, causing additional damage, forcing a decision to inactivate the towers. In 1963, TT2 was dismantled. The following year TT3 was also removed.

In 1989, the Berlin Wall came down. The Cold War that began four decades earlier had ended. Playing a role in the long road to victory were three radar stations off the east coast and the brave crews that served on their swaying platforms.

Nixon Takes Barnstable

After casting his vote in the 1960 presidential election at Boston on the morning of November 8, Senator John F. Kennedy and members of his entourage made the trek to Hyannis Port, arriving by midday. Joining him were his nine-month pregnant wife Jacqueline, daughter Caroline, parents Joseph and Rose, and brother Robert, who had earlier voted at Hyannis. Win or lose, JFK was expected to make a speech at the National Guard Armory on South Street later that evening.

Yet, as the evening progressed it became apparent that the vote was too close to call. Final results were not determined until the following day with Kennedy declared the victor. The nationwide popular vote margin was just 0.17%, or 113,000 votes over the total 68 million votes cast. Despite the narrow victory, the electoral vote was more revealing: Kennedy with 303 versus Nixon with 219. The election would prompt cries of voter fraud, particularly in Texas and Illinois, and demands that the Electoral College be scrapped. Despite the claims of fraud, Nixon decided against a recount, declaring, "Our country cannot afford the agony of a constitutional crisis."

On Wednesday afternoon, JFK's motorcade traveled from Hyannis Port up Sea Street, and along South Street to the Armory. There, the president-elect delivered his victory speech. Three hundred news reporters were at Hyannis to cover the event. Crowds of between 20,000 and 25,000 were expected, prompting all Barnstable police and 40 auxiliary policemen to report for duty. State Police presence was also felt throughout the area with some one hundred troopers mobilized. Kennedy remained on at Hyannis Port for the remainder of the week to rest up after months of campaigning.

Yet despite all the local hoopla, the Town of Barnstable and the village of Hyannis Port were not very kind to Kennedy on Election Day. Though the town saw a record voter turnout of 94%, it was Nixon who won locally with 4,515 votes to JFK's 2,783. Only the north precinct of Hyannis voted for Kennedy (857 votes to 783), while the south precinct of the village, which included Hyannis Port, went decisively to Nixon (1,024 to 733).

Cape Camelot
From 1961 to 1963, President Kennedy came to Hyannis Port to escape the pressures of Washington. In fact, he once remarked that he tended to visit the Cape when faced with a difficult decision.

Kennedy's connection with the Cape went back to the 1920's when his parents bought a summer place in Hyannis Port. It became a second home to JFK throughout his childhood and into his adult years. There he sailed his 26-foot Wianno Senior *Victura*, a gift from his 15th birthday. He later sailed it as Commander in Chief, once stating, "We are tied to the ocean. And when we go back to the sea—whether it is to sail or to watch it—we are going back from whence we came."

The May 18, 1961 issue of the *Barnstable Patriot* announced the possible arrival of the president: "There is a persistent rumor that (JFK) may stop over here on a return trip from Canada before he leaves for France." He did, in fact, visit Hyannis Port as document-ed with a front-page photograph of the President boarding his Air Force DC-6B at Barnstable Municipal Airport "after spending the holiday week end at the Hyannis Port home of his father, Joseph P. Kennedy." An accompanying article read, "President Kennedy's comings and goings this past holiday weekend created little more than a normal amount of traffic around the Town of Barnstable for a holiday period."

The following year, the Kennedys were again on Cape, as mentioned in the *Barnstable Patriot's* July 5 issue: "Kennedys continue to make the news, not only in Washington but right here at the airport ... Ted Kennedy, the president's brother has been coming and going ... The *Caroline* (the Kennedys' private plane) landed with Mrs. Ethel Kennedy, wife of Attorney General Robert Kennedy, and several of their children ... A day or so later Mrs. Rose Kennedy, the president's mother came in on Northeast Airlines from New York ... And more Kennedys are expected to arrive by air this weekend."

An editorial in the July 26, 1962 issue of the *Patriot* entitled "Please, Mr. President" opens a window on how the summer folk were perhaps viewing the invasion of the Kennedy clan and their entourage: "While the Kennedys frolic each weekend in Lewis Bay and other waters and the press have a heyday, many of the public who also enjoy their water sports are making sputtering noises not unlike that of a badly tuned motor."

Locally, the presence of the leader of the free world vacationing just down the road at Hyannis Port was seen as a seemingly every-day occurrence. Occasionally an airport update or editorial in the *Patriot* would shed some light on the Kennedys' activities. In fact, during one summer visit Kennedy didn't make the front page at all, though a story did run about a missing five-week old capuchin monkey named "Charlie" last seen in the West Barnstable area.

The national press, though, followed the president closely and they were there when on one July day JFK accidentally ran his *Victura* aground. The story ran coast to coast. "Whenever they put to sea ... they were followed by an armada of press boats, filled with photographers with telescopic lenses trying to record their oceanic adventures," wrote JFK's Press Secretary Pierre Salinger in his book *With Kennedy*.

"The flying Kennedys have launched the summer season with a flurry of air travel," announced the *Barnstable Patriot* at the beginning of what would be the president's last summer at Hyannis Port. The July 18, 1963 issue mentioned an incident involving a kite: "...we have it on very good authority that the kite launched from the Kennedy Flotilla last weekend was not the same kite which landed so inelegantly in the briney [sic] the weekend before. This particular kite had been purchased by the President and his son earlier in the day at a local emporium."

When not on Nantucket Sound, JFK could be found golfing at the Hyannis Port Club. According to Salinger he shot in the high 70's or low 80's , displaying "strong tee shots and deftness around the greens." Though Salinger added that Kennedy's long irons were "erratic."

Reverse Freedom Riders

In the early 1960's, the Kennedy administration began to support the desegregation of public establishments in southern states. In addition to the effort at the national level, there was a ground swell of participation led by northern liberals that led to the famous "Freedom Rides" that took civil rights protesters all across Dixie. Hundreds of students, academics, and religious leaders descended on the south to register black voters and speed up the progress of civil rights.

The reaction of the white communities in the South was any-thing but sympathetic. In an ironic and cruel reaction to the efforts of northerners to force the issue of equality on the South, segrega-tionists hit on a plan to embarrass President Kennedy in his own backyard. They decided to bus blacks north to Hyannis where Kennedy maintained his summer home. Enticed with free tickets and promises of jobs in Massachusetts, a number of poor blacks accepted what they believed to be a genuine offer of a better life. When the riders from the South arrived on Cape Cod there was bewilderment, anger, and eventually an effort to try and deal with what was a very real human problem.

The first group of "Reverse Freedom Riders," as they were termed by the press, arrived in Hyannis in May of 1962. The majority came from Little Rock, Arkansas. But the group also included people from the states of Louisiana and Georgia. Over a three-week period, almost fifty destitute black citizens arrived at the bus depot on Barnstable Road. They all had been told that the people of Cape Cod had paid for their fares and that representatives of the local government would meet them and offer jobs. It was a cruel hoax perpetrated on these poor people. None of the story was true. Dr. Irving Bartlett, then president of Cape Cod Community College, assisted the new arrivals, many of them with children, in getting temporary housing at the South Street campus of Cape Cod Community College.

"They lied to us about being met by a representative of the president's cabinet and that jobs were awaiting us here," said William Ricks of Little Rock. Mrs. Lila Mae Williams said that she had been told in Little Rock that she would be able to support her nine children as a domestic worker in Massachusetts. There were many similar stories.

Segregationists in the South took huge pleasure at what was happening in Hyannis. Amis Guthridge, president of the white supremacist Little Rock Capital Citizens Council, said that his group would continue to send blacks to Massachusetts and to other areas in the North, "until northern politicians stop agitating us with so-called civil rights legislation."

A group of Cape Codders immediately began working for the welfare of the Reverse Freedom Riders. It was clear that segregationists had targeted the poor and unskilled in their scheme. Reverend Ken Warren, pastor of the Barnstable Unitarian Church, headed up a local citizens committee, which included John Rosario, Eugenia Fortes, and Dan Serpico, and this group began to organize donations of food, clothing, and bedding for the stranded bus riders. The group, which called itself the Cape Cod Refugee Relief Committee, suggested that the riders might be better housed at Otis Air Force Base. By June, some of the blacks were able to move to the military facility where they found temporary quarters. Civic groups across the Cape were asked to help in finding permanent housing and jobs. But it was a difficult task. Unemployment on

Cape Cod during the off-season in those days regularly reached as high as 20% of the population and there was clearly no market for unskilled workers beyond the ten-week summer season.

Largely because of this, the great majority of blacks moved away from Cape Cod where there were better job opportunities. A number of them eventually returned to their former homes in the South. One family that stayed in Hyannis was that of Virginia Bell. With eleven children, she had known the hardship of poverty in Arkansas and she had no thoughts of ever turning back. She found work, at first in a laundry, and eventually at the hospital as a nurse's aid. Years later she acknowledged that for her, at least, the reverse freedom ride had been a success. "They were so nice to me, so good to me, and they've been so good to me ever since," she recalled. As with so many others who have come to these shores as refugees of one sort or another, Virginia Bell overcame great odds and became a symbol of the resiliency of the human spirit.

November 1963

The November 21, 1963 issue of the weekly *Barnstable Patriot* tells a story of normal life in the town, with no indication of the historic day to follow. Schools would be letting out at mid-day on the following Wednesday for Thanksgiving. Turkeys at the First National Food Store were advertised at 39 cents per pound. A Friday night rally was scheduled to support the Barnstable Red Raiders in their annual Thanksgiving Day football game against Falmouth. The Cape Symphony Orchestra was scheduled to perform with soloist Beverly Sills while the Barnstable Comedy Club was presenting *Death of a Salesman*. Barnstable hockey tryouts were to take place on Saturday morning at the Kennedy Skating Rink. Little did anyone know that normal life would be disrupted by gunshots in Dallas upon the following day.

The next week's *Patriot*—published on Thanksgiving, November 28—told a much different story. It was the story of a town described as "emotionally exhausted and sorrowful."

"With heavy hearts, stunned by the shock of last Friday's terrible tragedy, the people of the Town of Barnstable went on with the business of putting Thanksgiving together ... The people of the town, many of whom knew Jack Kennedy well since his boyhood summers at Hyannis Port, are striving to resume a normal pattern of living after weary days and nights in front of television sets or next to radios ... But the void that is so great this Thanksgiving across the nation and in many foreign lands is, of course, deepest within the Compound at Hyannis Port. To no small degree do the townspeople share that void, for Barnstable was, indeed, Jack Kennedy's summer home town."

"He was courageous not only in battles of foreign wars, but in the battles of equality for all men, without regard for race, creed, color, or birth," said Rev. Leonard J. Daley of St. Francis Xavier, where the Kennedy family worshiped.

"The things for which he worked, planned and prayed are indelibly marked on the hearts of each American," added Rev. John A. Bankosky of the West Parish Meetinghouse. While Rabbi Jerome Pine of the Cape Cod Synagogue said, "We will not cry out for vengeance for blood and exact it as one man has done ... for this would desecrate our late President's memory." And from Dr. Carl F. Schultz of the Federated Church of Hyannis: "The late John F. Kennedy will be remembered as one who cherished the ideals of freedom, liberty and justice for all, of peace and brotherhood. He worked for them. He gave his life for them."

Plans were discussed to erect a memorial in Barnstable to honor the fallen president. A committee, "acting on the unanimous special town meeting approval," was named by the Board of Selectmen for that purpose. The result was the John F. Kennedy Memorial on Ocean Street in Hyannis, overlooking Lewis Bay. The bas-relief memorial with its accompanying fountain was opened to the public in 1966.

West Falmouth's Pink Granite

When people think about Cape Cod, sand fills their thoughts as well as their shoes. Dig a hole in the ground just about anywhere and within a few feet you will strike sand—lots of it. With the exception of the Cape's north side—and its stonewalls—there are few rocks of any size anywhere south of the mid-Cape highway. Geologists tell us that the solid base of bedrock is between 250 and 450 feet below the surface, above which is sand and clay. But in one part of the upper Cape large pieces of granite in the glacial debris

along Route 28A were once the basis for a local stone cutting industry. That area is West Falmouth.

Over the years the granite boulders in the hills above West
Falmouth gave employment to several local stone cutters who used
the hard stone in building foundations and rock walls along Route
28A. In the mid-1800's, there were two stonecutters registered in
Falmouth. At the end of the century that number had doubled.
Candace Jenkins, in her book, *Between the Forest and Bay - A History
of West Falmouth as Revealed in its Historic Buildings and Landscapes*,
mentions Seth Gifford, Mayhew Stuart, Daniel Weeks, and
Theodore Burdick as practicing stone masons in the town around
1900. Their legacy can be seen in the many dressed stonewalls and
foundations along what locals refer to as West Falmouth Highway.
Several buildings survive from the nineteenth century that were at
least in part built from rocks taken out of the hills above
Chapaquoit Harbor. One of these, a barn built by Daniel Weeks,
shows graceful arched door openings in the lower sections of
the building. It is a substantial structure by any standards. A
second, just south of the West Falmouth Library, has a longer
history as a blacksmith shop and has been in continuous use since
the eighteenth century.

John F. Kennedy Gravesite, Arlington, Virginia. (Jim Coogan photo)

Often the Cape Cod strain of granite is referred to as "pink granite." This is not evident in the ubiquitous rock walls and foundations in the area, but it can be seen in certain local cemetery stones and in a few ornamental thresholds. One of the important but lesser known applications of West Falmouth's pink granite is in the John F. Kennedy gravesite in Arlington National Cemetery in Virginia.

William Milhomme, Field Archaeologist for the Massachusetts Archives in Boston, tracked down the story of how pieces of Cape granite ended up at the Kennedy gravesite. He passed the information along to Mary Sicchio, archivist at the William Brewster Nickerson historical collection at Cape Cod Community College.

During the Camelot years, Jacqueline Kennedy used to frequent a number of antique shops along Route 28A when she was vacationing on Cape Cod. One of her favorite shops was the Antiquarian in Falmouth, owned by Orville Garland. Mrs. Kennedy's relationship with the Garland shop existed over a number of years, both before and after her husband's assassination. In 1964, after choosing the architectural firm of John Warnecke and Associates to design and build President Kennedy's memorial at Arlington, Mrs. Kennedy contacted Garland to see if he might be able to procure some pink granite, similar to a piece that was part of the entranceway to the antique shop. She wanted it incorporated into the memorial.

Garland contacted Dick Baker, who owned Baker Monument Company in Falmouth. Baker's business of tearing down some of the older houses in the area had left him with a considerable amount of demolition debris. A collection of stone from old fireplaces, chimneys, and foundations was stockpiled on Baker's property. There was even an old millstone. Without telling Baker what he wanted the granite for, Garland made the purchase and arranged for it to be shipped to Robert and Ethel Kennedy's estate, Hickory Hill, located in McLean, Virginia. Robert Kennedy had a mason cut the granite remnants to the specifications of John Warnecke, the architect.

The Kennedy Memorial was begun in 1965 and completed in 1967. In addition to the president, two of his children who had predeceased him—Patrick Bouvier Kennedy and an unnamed

stillborn daughter—were interred at the completed site. In May of
1994, Jacqueline Kennedy was interred next to President Kennedy.
The family now rests together near the eternal flame, surrounded
by pieces of Cape Cod from the hills of West Falmouth.

Hurricane of '91: A Blowhard Named Bob!

The 20th century sent a handful of strong hurricanes to our New
England shores, the greatest of which was the Hurricane of 1938.
That storm came and left very quickly on the afternoon of
September 21. In her wake she left some 600 people dead and the
equivalent of $3.5 billion in damage throughout the northeast. The
hurricane of 1944 followed six years later and caused more damage.

The year 1954 brought the one-two punch of hurricanes Carol
on August 21 and Edna less than two weeks later. Another hurricane, Connie, arrived during the very next year, shutting down the
Barnstable County Fair early and sending tourists packing.
Hurricane Donna arrived on September 12, 1960, causing damage
equivalent to $1.8 billion. Seasoned Cape Codders recall these
hurricanes, and speak of them with a wary eye cast toward the
Atlantic, as if awaiting the next tempest.

For those relative newcomers to Cape Cod, Hurricane Bob of
1991 is the one they remember. Though only a Category 2 storm
(on a scale from 1 to 5), it is still remembered locally for the damage and power outages it caused. Throughout New England it was
responsible for eleven deaths and some $1.5 billion in destruction.

The storm began life on August 15 as a tropical depression off
the Bahamas and by the next day wind speeds reached 40 miles per
hour, prompting an upgrade to a tropical storm. The storm reached
hurricane status over the following two days as wind speeds
exceeded 75 miles per hour. Over that time, it had traveled northwest about two hundred miles off the Florida coast. It then raced
north at 40 miles per hour, reaching the northeast coast early on the
afternoon of August 19 with maximum wind speeds of 115 miles
per hour. These speeds decreased to 90 miles per hour by landfall,
which occurred about 50 miles west of Cape Cod. Being east of the
eye, the Cape was subjected to the hurricane's strongest winds
though little in terms of rainfall. In fact, throughout much of the
Cape less than a quarter inch of precipitation was reported.

The damage was widespread along the Cape with boats piling up in south facing harbors and tree damage everywhere and in most every village. Along Route 6A, hundred-year-old trees were uprooted while elsewhere shore roads were flooded by the storm surge. Seaside hotels saw damage, business signs were blown down, and homes were damaged here and there by fallen trees and flying debris. Destroyed was the new addition to the First Congregational Church of Falmouth. In Hyannis the Melody Tent was toppled, causing cancellations throughout the following weeks.

Repair crews from as far away as Ohio, North Carolina, and even Canada were called in to fix downed power lines as some locals went for up to a week without electricity. Ice suddenly became valuable as food spoiled. Grocery store shelves grew bare. Milk, bread, and batteries became the necessities of life. Without electricity, a battery-powered radio was the Cape Codders' lifeline to the outside world, recalling a more "primitive" time.

Prior to the hurricane's arrival, tourists packed up and left. Local businesses suffered, with the remaining weeks of the summer season used instead to repair damage. The drone of chainsaws became a common sound as an army of work crews from off Cape cleared away fallen limbs. Meanwhile, the sight of the National Guard on local roads lent the Cape a military air during the weeks following the hurricane.

Strangely, trees that didn't topple during the storm had their leaves turn autumnal colors early due to the wind-driven ocean salt. By September most trees were bare, robbing the fall season of its normal brilliance. Some trees began to re-bud as the cycle of the seasons was disturbed.

The worst destruction was witnessed along the coast, and particularly at the harbors. Boats were tossed and smashed in a carnage that bordered on something unworldly. The damage at Lewis Bay was absolute, with whole boats and pieces of boats cast up on land. At East Bay in Osterville some vessels were tossed more than 500 feet inland—a bow here, a stern there, unidentifiable pieces scattered everywhere. It was a nautical scene not witnessed around these parts since the turn of the 20th century when ships wrecked along the outer Cape coastline with regularity.

The events of August 19, 1991 and the days that followed have now become part of Cape Cod's history and lore. Years from now, stories of "Bob," the Hurricane of '91, will be told in the same breath as the stories of other great storms to arrive along these outermost shores.

The Man Who Stopped the Rain

Mashpee has had its share of legendary personalities down through the centuries. In the 17th century, Simon Popmonet served as Mashpee's first Native preacher. In the 18th century, Reuben Cognehew traveled to England to discuss the plight of the Mashpee Indians before King George III. And in the 19th century, William Apes, a Native Indian preacher from the Pequot tribe, settled in Mashpee and, with the help of Baptist minister "Blind" Joe Amos, drew up resolutions for home rule.

Yet, it is not necessary to go back centuries in order to find important figures in Mashpee's proud history. The 20th century produced John Peters, known also by his Native name— Cjegktoonuppa—meaning Slow Turtle. Born in 1930, Slow Turtle learned the Native customs at an early age. His training and his dedication to his people's way of life led to him becoming supreme medicine man of the Wampanoag Nation. He once stated, "I am charged and empowered to practice the ancestral spiritual teachings of my People. These teachings have been handed down from generation to generation to express our relation to All That Is."

Peters was an advocate who worked tirelessly to secure the rights of fellow Native Americans, as well as for all people. His work also included preserving the culture of the Wampanoag and other tribes, and in fact he was executive director of the Massachusetts' Commission on Indian Affairs, a position he held for more than 20 years. His efforts brought about the American Indian Religious Freedom Act and the Indian Child Welfare Act, which houses Native Indian orphans in Native homes in order to foster cultural teachings and upbringing. Also, Peters' work resulted in the Native American Graves Repatriation Act. This important piece of legislation ensures that remains from digs, museums, and institutions are returned to their respective tribe for reburial.

On a more spiritual level, it is said that Slow Turtle twice caused the rain to stop falling. One time it happened on Cape Cod before a crowd and on another occasion during a trip to Japan. When he was once asked to offer up a prayer to ensure fair weather for an outdoor event, Slow Turtle responded, "Every day is a good day. You need rain, you need sun, wind to blow things around. Every day is a good day."

Slow Turtle's earthly days ended in November 1997. Following a ceremony at the Old Indian Cemetery in Mashpee, his ashes were scattered off South Cape Beach. The circle of Slow Turtle's purposeful life was now complete.

Acknowledgments

It is fair to ask where all these stories about Cape Cod came from. First, there were the old Brewster families that were part of my childhood—the Clarks, Pratts, Bakers, Fosters, Doanes, Bassetts, Crockers, Chases, and Crosbys. In my grade school years, they filled me with ancestral tales and they gave me a love of the Cape's history. As a teenager, working summers for the highway department, I had the chance to get to know some real characters who added to the store of stories that have stayed with me into my adult years. Hollis "Tiny" Theall, Leslie "Let" Chase, Dennis Dugan, and Harry "Mutt" Alexander were a veritable store house of yarns. I absorbed them all. The late Walter Babbitt, who served as Brewster town archivist, was a friend and mentor who could always run down a fact when I needed it. Washington Irving "Poet" Eldredge, Robbie Hooper, and Joshua Crowell, all old friends now passed on, were other sources.

Additional stories in this book came from libraries and archives. Perhaps my most enjoyable days are spent in places like the Sturgis Public Library in Barnstable and the William Brewster Nickerson Special Collections Room at the Cape Cod Community College. Historical societies across the Cape should also be thanked for their permission to use materials and photographs to support each chapter in *Cape Cod Harvest*.

Finally, there are people who deserve special mention. Mary Sicchio, archivist at the Community College Nickerson Room, has never failed to find information that could help me fill out a story. Her predecessor, Charlotte Price, was equally helpful. I thank them both. Sandwich resident, Linda Haller, was a most thorough and helpful proofreader of the manuscript. Jack Sheedy continues to be a wonderful writing partner and a valued friend. Jackie Rockwell of Rockwell Design has once again given this newest of our books a professional and attractive look. Finally, and perhaps most important, I must credit my wife Beth for having the love and patience to let me follow all of my dreams.

John Coogan

My message of acknowledgment begins with an immeasurable thank you to my family. My wife, Adriana, has been hugely supportive of my work over the years and I often rely on her advice and proofreading abilities as I near deadline. My children, Melissa and Gregory, have grown up with the sound of their Dad tapping away at the keyboard, and they've always provided me with quiet moments in which to work. A big thank you goes to my sister-in-law, and graphic designer, Jackie Rockwell, who put this book together from front cover to back cover . . . and everything in between . . . making our written words that much more appealing.

Thanks also to Rob Sennott, publisher of the *Barnstable Patriot*, for his continuing support and friendship. I wish to recognize the many libraries across the Cape, particularly in Dennis, Brewster, Harwich, Barnstable, and at Cape Cod Community College, and the librarians who have always pointed me in the right direction. Thanks also to the historical societies and museums I've visited from the Cape tip to the canal. And I offer my sincere gratitude to Jim Coogan—my co-author, my publisher, and my dear friend. We have shared many good times over the past eight years since the publication of our first book together—*Cape Cod Companion*. He has always been in my corner, providing brotherly advice, sometimes over a cup of chowder or a cup of coffee, and for that I am eternally grateful.

About the Authors

Jim Coogan was raised in Brewster in the home where famed Cape Cod author Joseph Crosby Lincoln was born. Just as Lincoln absorbed the classic flavor of that seafaring town and applied his observations in his many novels, so also does Jim write about Cape Cod from his vantage point of almost 60 years of living in this very special place. A retired high school history teacher, he is a popular lecturer and a regular columnist for the *Cape Cod Times* daily newspaper. His book, *Sail Away Ladies: Stories of Cape Cod Women in the Age of Sail*, won the 2004 United States Maritime Literature Award for best sea-related book by an independent publisher. *Cape Cod Harvest* is his third collaboration with Dennis author Jack Sheedy. Jim lives in Sandwich, Massachusetts with his wife Elizabeth and their Great Dane, Sussannah.

Jack Sheedy is the author of five books and more than 500 published articles. His books include *Cape Cod Companion* and *Cape Cod Voyage*, written with Jim Coogan. Jack has served as a freelance writer for the *Barnstable Patriot* newspaper for more than 20 years, also serving as managing editor of its annual history magazine *Summerscape*—issues of this publication have been recognized by the New England Press Association for editorial excellence. He is a contributor to *Cape Cod Life* magazine and other Cape publications, and has written copy for a number of Cape businesses and organizations as well as for the John F. Kennedy Library in Boston. Jack has appeared on HGTV and NPR radio, speaking about Cape Cod history and lore. Spending summers in Dennisport since childhood, Jack, his wife Adriana, and their children have lived in Dennis for the past 20 years.

Bibliography

Andrews, H. Franklin. *The Hamlin Family: A Genealogy of James Hamlin of Barnstable, Massachusetts.* Exira, Iowa. Published privately by the author, 1902.

Apess, William. *Son of the Forest.* Amherst, MA: University of Massachusetts Press, 1997.

Arber, Edward, Ed. *The Story of the Pilgrim Fathers, 1606-1623 A.D., As Told by Themselves, Their Friends, and Their Enemies.* London: Houghton Mifflin & Co., 1897.

Archer, Gleason L. *With Axe and Musket at Plymouth.* New York, NY: The American Historical Society, Inc., 1936.

Barnard, Ruth L. *A History of Orleans.* Taunton, MA: William S. Sullwold Publishing, 1975.

Barnstable County. *Three Centuries of a Cape Cod County: Barnstable, Massachusetts, 1685-1985.* Barnstable, MA: Barnstable County, 1985.

Bingham, Amelia. *Mashpee: Land of the Wampanoags.* Mashpee, MA: Mashpee Centennial Committee, 1970.

Bloom Arthur. *Joseph Jefferson: Dean of the American Theatre.* Savannah, GA: Frederic C. Bell Publisher, Inc., 2000

Bodensiek, Fred. *Barnstable at 350.* Barnstable, MA: Barnstable 350th Committee, 1989.

Bowles, Francis Tiffany. *The Loyalty of Barnstable in the Revolution.* Reprinted from the publications of the Colonial Society of Massachusetts, Vol. XXV. Cambridge, MA: John Wilson & Son, The University Press, 1924.

Bradford, William. *Bradford's History "of Plymouth Plantation."* Boston, MA: Wright & Potter Printing Co, 1898.

Brigham, Albert Perry. *Cape Cod and the Old Colony.* New York, NY: Grosset & Dunlap, 1920.

Bunnelle, Philip. *The New England Ancestry of George R. Perry, 1867-1947.* Santa Clara, CA: Privately printed, 1998.

Burrows, Fredrika A. *Windmills of Cape Cod and Islands.* Taunton, MA: William Sullwold Publishing, Inc., 1978.

Burns, Rosemary H. *Mashpee - 125 Anniversary.* Mashpee, MA: Town of Mashpee, 1995.

Butterworth Company. *Cape Cod & Islands Atlas.* West Yarmouth, MA.

Carpenter, Delores Bird. *Early Encounters.* East Lansing, MI: Michigan State University Press, 1994.

Carpenter, Edmund J., *The Pilgrims and Their Monument*. New York, NY: D. Appleton and Co., 1911.

Clark, Admont G. *They Built Clipper Ships in Their Back Yard*. Yarmouthport, MA: Parnassus Imprint, 1963.

Corbett, Scott. *We Chose Cape Cod*. New York, NY: Thomas Y. Crowell Co, 1953.

Cousy, Bob & Al Hirshberg. *Basketball is My Life*. Englewood Cliffs, N.J: Prentice Hall, Inc., 1957.

Cropsey, Eugene H. *Crosby's Opera House: Symbol of Chicago's Cultural Awakening*. Published by Associated University Presses, Inc., 1999.

Crosby, Katharine. *Blue-Water Men & Other Cape Codders*. New York, NY: The Macmillan Company, 1946.

Delores Bird, Ed. *Early Encounters: Native Americans and Europeans in New England*. From the papers of W. Sears Nickerson. East Lansing, MI: Michigan State University Press, 1994.

Dana, Julian. *Gods Who Die: The Story of Samoa's Greatest Adventurer, as told to Julian Dana*. New York, NY: The Macmillan Company, 1935.

Dean, Nicholas. *Snow Squall: The Last American Clipper Ship*. Gardiner, ME: Tilbury House, Publishers, 2001.

Deetz, James and Patricia. *The Times of Their Lives: Life, Love, and Death in Plymouth Colony*. New York, NY: W.H. Freeman & Co., 2000.

Deyo, Simeon L. *History of Barnstable County, Massachusetts 1620-1890*. New York, NY: H.W. Blake & Co, 1890.

Digges, Jeremiah (Josef Berger). *Cape Cod Pilot*. Provincetown, MA & New York, NY: Modern Pilgrim Press and Viking Press, 1937.

Dow, George Francis. *Everyday Life in the Massachusetts Bay Colony*. Boston, MA: Society for the Preservation of New England Antiquities, 1935.

Ellis, James. *Mad Jack Percival: Legend of the Old Navy*. Annapolis, MD: Naval Institute Press, 2002.

Ellis, Lester N. *The True Story of a Master Mariner*. Philadelphia, PA: Dorrance & Company, 1969.

Fawsett, Marise. *Cape Cod Annals*. Bowie, MD: Heritage Books, Inc., 1990.

Farson, Robert. *The Cape Cod Canal*. Middletown, CT: Wesleyan University Press, 1977.

Fay, Joseph Story. *Woods Holl: The Track of the Norseman. A Monograph by Joseph Story Fay of Woods Holl, Massachusetts*. Boston, MA: Wright & Potter Printing Co., 1882.

Freeman, Frederick. *The History of Cape Cod*. Yarmouth Port, MA: Parnassus Imprints, 1965.

Fritze, Hattie Blossom. *Horse & Buggy Days on Old Cape Cod*. Barnstable, MA: Great Marshes Press, 1966.

Gamble, Adam. *1880 Atlas of Barnstable County*. Yarmouthport, MA: On Cape Publications, 1998.

Geoffrey, Theodate. *Suckanesset: Wherein May be Read a History of Falmouth Massachusetts*. Falmouth, MA: Falmouth Publishing Co., 1928, pages 64-66.

Gibson, Marjorie Hubbell. *Historical & Genealogical Atlas and Guide to Barnstable County*. Teaticket, MA: Falmouth Genealogical Society, 1995.

Gibson, Marjorie Hubbell. *H.M.S. Somerset: 1746-1778*. Cotuit, MA: Abbey Gate House, 1992.

Green, Eugene and William Sachse. *Names of the Land*. Chester, CT: Globe Pequot Press, 1983.

Griffis, William Elliot. *The Pilgrims in Their Three Homes*. New York, NY: Houghton, Mifflin & Co., 1898.

Halberstam, David. *The Fifties*. New York, NY: Villard Books. 1993.

Hale, E. E. *Stories of the Sea*. Boston, MA: Roberts Brothers, 1880.

Harris, Charles E. *Hyannis Sea Captains*. Hyannis, MA: The Register Press, 1939.

Hassell, Martha. *The Challenge of Hannah Rebecca*. Sandwich, MA: Sandwich Historical Society, 1986.

Higgins, Katharine Chapin. *Richard Higgins and His Descendants*. Worcester, MA: privately printed, 1913.

Hodges, Margaret. *Hopkins of the Mayflower: Portrait of a Dissenter*. New York, NY: Farrar, Straus, and Giroux, 1972.

Howe, Octavius T. & Frederick C. Matthews. *American Clipper Ships 1833-1858, Volumes I & II*. New York, NY: Dover Publications, Inc., 1986 edition.

Hurd, Edith Thacher. *The Wreck of the Wild Wave: Being the True Account of the Clipper Ship Wild Wave of Boston*. New York, NY: Oxford University Press, 1942.

Jalbert, Russel R. *Where Sea & History Meet - 4000 Years of Life in Orleans*. Orleans, MA: Orleans Bicentennial Commission, 1997.

Jennings, Herman A. *Provincetown: Or Odds and Ends From the Tip End*. Provincetown, MA: Reprint edition by Peaked Hill Press, 1995 (Original printing in 1890).

Keene, Betsey D. *History of Bourne from 1622 to 1937*. Yarmouthport, MA: Charles W. Swift, 1937.

King, H. Roger. *Cape Cod & Plymouth Colony in the Seventeenth Century*. Lanham, MD: University Press of America, 1994.

Kittredge, Henry C. *Cape Cod: Its People & Their History*. Boston, MA: Houghton Mifflin Company, 1968.

Kittredge, Henry C. *Mooncussers of Cape Cod*. New York, NY: Houghton Mifflin Co., 1937.

Kittredge, Henry C. *Shipmasters of Cape Cod*. Boston, MA & New York, NY: Houghton Mifflin Company, 1935.

Lawson, Evelyn. *Yesterday's Cape Cod*. Miami, FL: E.A. Seemann Publishing, Inc., 1975.

Lee, Helen Bourne Joy. *The Bourne Genealogy*. Pequot Press, 1972.

Lincoln, Joseph C. *Cape Cod Yesterdays*. New York, NY: Blue Ribbon Books, 1939.

Lincoln, Joseph C. *Rugged Water*. New York, NY: D. Appleton and Company, 1924.

Lombardo, Dan. *Windmills of New England: Their Genius, Madness, History, and Future*. Yarmouth Port, MA: On Cape Publications, 2003.

Long, David F. *"Mad Jack" The Biography of Captain John Persival USN 1779-1862*. Westport, CT: Greenwood Press, 1993.

Lovell, Jr., R.A. *Sandwich—A Cape Cod Town*. Sandwich, MA: Town of Sandwich Archives & Historical Center, 1984.

Lowe, Alice A. *Nauset on Cape Cod - A History of Eastham*. Eastham, MA: Eastham Historical Society, 1968.

Martin, Alverta Brown. *Albert Crosby, A Family History*. Rowland Heights, CA: Privately printed, 1977.

May, Samuel P. *Descendants of Richard Sears of Yarmouth, Massachusetts, 1638-1888.* Albany, NY: Joel Munsell's Sons, 1890.

Miller, Pamela A. *And the Whale is Ours: Creative Writing of American Whalemen.* Salem, MA: David R.Godine, Publisher. The Kendall Whaling Museum, 1979.

Mjelde, Michael Jay. *Glory of the Seas.* Middletown, CT: Wesleyan University Press (published for the Marine Historical Association), 1970.

Monbleau, Marcia J. *The Cape Playhouse.* South Yarmouth, MA: Allen D. Bragdon Publishers, Inc., 1991.

Moses, George. *Ring Around the Punchbowl: The Story of Beebe Woods in Falmouth on Cape Cod.* Taunton, MA: W.S. Sullwold Publishers, 1976.

Nickerson 2nd, Joshua Atkins. *Days to Remember.* Chatham, MA: Chatham Historical Society, 1988.

O'Neil, Neva. *Master Mariners of Dennis.* Dennis, MA: Dennis Historical Society, 1965.

Otis, Amos. *Genealogical Notes of Barnstable Families.* Barnstable, MA: F.B. & F.P. Goss Publishers and Printers, 1888.

Price, Christopher. *Baseball by the Beach: A History of America's National Pastime on Cape Cod.* Hyannis, MA: Parnassus Imprints, 1998.

Quinn, William. *Cape Cod Maritime Disasters.* Orleans, MA: Lower Cape Publishing, 1990.

Reid, Nancy Thacher. *Dennis, Cape Cod.* Dennis, MA: Dennis Historical Society, 1996.

Reynard, Elizabeth. *The Narrow Land.* Chatham, MA: Chatham Historical Society, 1978.

Ryder, Marion Crowell. *Cape Cod Remembrances.* Taunton, MA: William S. Sullwold Publishing, 1972.

Salinger, Pierre. *With Kennedy.* Garden City, NY: Doubleday, 1966.

Sawyer, Richard, Ed. *From Pocasset to Cataumet: The Origins of a Massachusetts Seaside Community.* Bourne, MA: Bourne Historical Commission, 1988.

Sears, J. Henry. *Brewster Ship Masters.* Yarmouth Port, MA: C. W. Swift, 1906.

Schlesinger, Jr., Arthur M. *Robert Kennedy and His Times.* Boston, MA: Houghton Mifflin, 1978.

Small, Isaac M. *Shipwrecks on Cape Cod.* Chatham, MA: The Chatham Press, Inc., 1967.

Smith, Leonard, Ed. *Barnstable Town Records as printed in Cape Cod Library of Local History and Genealogy, Vol. 2.* Baltimore, MD: Genealogical Publishing Co., Inc., 1992.

Smith, Mary Lou. *Woods Hole Reflections.* Woods Hole, MA: Woods Hole Historical Association, 1983.

Smith, Mary Lou. *The Book of Falmouth: A Tercentennial Celebration 1686-1986.* Falmouth, MA: Falmouth Historical Society, 1986

Smith, William C. *A History of Chatham, Massachusetts.* Chatham, MA: Chatham Historical Society., 1971 edition.

Snow, Edward Rowe. *A Pilgrim Returns to Cape Cod.* Boston, MA: The Yankee Publishing Co., 1946.

Swift, Charles F. *History of Old Yarmouth.* Yarmouthport, MA: The Historical Society of Old Yarmouth, 1975.

Tarbell, Arthur Wilson. *Cape Cod Ahoy.* Boston, MA: A.T. Ramsay and Co, 1932.

Tarbell, Arthur W. *I Retire to Cape Cod.* New York, N.Y: Stephen Daye, Inc., 1944.

Thoreau, Henry David. *Cape Cod.* New York, NY: Bramhall House, 1951.

Town of Barnstable. *The Seven Villages of Barnstable.* Barnstable, MA: Town of Barnstable, 1976.

Trayser, Donald G. *Barnstable: Three Centuries of a Cape Cod Town.* Hyannis, MA: F.B. & F.P. Goss, 1939.

Various authors including Dr. A. Lawrence Lovell and Donald G. Trayser. *Cotuit—Some Notes on Her History.* Hyannis, MA: F.B. & F.P. Goss, 1939.

Vorse, Mary Heaton. *Time and the Town: A Provincetown Chronicle.* New York, NY: Dial Press, 1942.

Vuilleumier, Marion. *Cape Cod - A Pictorial History.* Norfolk, VA: The Donning Co., 1982.

Vuilleumier, Marion. *Indians on Olde Cape Cod.* Taunton, MA: Wm. S. Sullwold Publishing, 1970.

Vuilleumier, Marion. *Sketches of Old Cape Cod.* Taunton, MA: Wm. S. Sullwold Publishing, 1972.

Vuilleumier, Marion. *The Town of Yarmouth, Massachusetts - A History: 1639-1989.* Yarmouth, MA: The Historical Society of Old Yarmouth, 1989.

Ward, R. Gerald. *American Activities in the Central Pacific 1790-1870.* Ridgewood, NJ: Gregg Press, Volume II.

Watters, Gerry Geddes Buss. *Privateers, Pirates, and Beyond: Memoirs of Lucy Lord Howes Hooper 1862-1863 and 1866-1909.* Dennis, MA: Dennis Historical Society, 2003.

Williams, Harold. *One Whaling Family.* Boston, MA: Houghton Mifflin Co., 1964.

Willison, George P. *Saints & Strangers.* New York, NY: Time, Inc. 1964.

Wilson, Harold C. *Gosnold's Hope: The Story of Bartholomew Gosnold.* Greenboro, NC: Tudor Publishers, 2000.

Wood, William. *New England's Prospect.* Amherst, MA: University of Massachusetts Press, 1977.

Yarmouth Historical Commission. *Yarmouth—Old Homes and Gathering Places.* Yarmouth, MA, 1989.

Young, Henry James. *George Eldridge, Hydrographer and Eliza Jane His Wife: Their Ancestors and Their Descendants.* Carlisle, PA: privately published, 1982.

Periodicals:

Boston Sunday Globe, "Recalling the unlikely journey of Rockwell Kent," by Christine Temin, August 6, 2000, page N12.

Boston Sunday Globe, "Saving a celestial vision," by Brian MacQuarrie, August 15, 1999, page C1.

Cape Cod Times, "Toleration of the tavern," by Jim Coogan, May 9, 1985, page 39.

Cape Cod Times, "Rockwell Kent: The man behind the Dennis mural," by Loren King, August 16, 2003, page C1

Cape Cod Magazine, "Winter Sports on Long Pond," by Robert H. Cahoon, Wareham, MA., March, 1916, pages 6,7.

The Cape magazine, "Amos Was a Real Bohemian," Orleans, MA: Nauset Publishers Inc., 1967, page 25.

New York Times, MacFayden obituary, August 27, 1972.

Associated Press, October 29, 1997
Barnstable Patriot, July 9, 1834.
Barnstable Patriot, May 23, 1849.
Barnstable Patriot, March 19, 1861.
Barnstable Patriot, April 28, 1863.
Barnstable Patriot, November 3, 1960
Barnstable Patriot, November 10, 1960
Barnstable Patriot, May 18, 1961
Barnstable Patriot, June 1, 1961
Barnstable Patriot, July 5, 1962
Barnstable Patriot, July 19, 1962
Barnstable Patriot, July 26, 1962
Barnstable Patriot, June 27, 1963
Barnstable Patriot, July 18, 1963
Barnstable Patriot, August 1, 1963
Barnstable Patriot, November 21, 1963
Barnstable Patriot, November 28, 1963
Barnstable Patriot, December 5, 1963
Barnstable Patriot, August 22, 1991
Barnstable Patriot, (Summerscape), June 1996
Barnstable Patriot, August 26, 1999
Barnstable Patriot, February 17, 2000
Boston Herald, May 30, 1962
Boston Record American, May 29, 1962
Boston Daily Evening Transcript, January 13, 1853
Cape Cod Standard Times, July 23, 1959, page 1
Cape Cod Standard Times, June 12, 1962
Cape Cod Times, May 17, 1992
Cape Cod Times, November 2, 1997
Cape Cod Times, February 8, 1999
Falmouth Enterprise, October 26, 1945.
Falmouth Enterprise, December 28, 1945.
The Friend Magazine, October 1863, page 76
Nautical Magazine, 1858, pages 453-54.
Provincetown Advocate, July 23, 1959, page 2
The Register, June 26, 1926.
Yarmouth Register, January 21, 1861, page 2.
Yarmouth Register, March 15, 1861
Yarmouth Register, November 7, 1862.
Yarmouth Register, May 20, 1864
Yarmouth Register, October 26, 1875.
Yarmouth Register, November 2, 1875.
Yarmouth Register, March 4, 1905
Yarmouth Register, March 11, 1905
Yarmouth Register, January 27, 1906

Yarmouth Register, January 17, 1925
Yarmouth Register May 26, 1932

Websites:
www.presidentkennedy.com
www.nationaltrust.org
www.musicexpert.com
www.grammyawards.com/awards
www.rense.com
www.texastowers.com
www.controlled-demolition.com
www.deepexplorers.com
www.njscuba.com
www.wahoo2001.com
www.dean-boys.com
www.state.ma.us
www.celehahn.org
www.plimoth.org
www.teachervision.com
www.vineyard.net
www.britainexpress.com
www.geocities.com
www.famousamericans.net

www.library.upenn.edu
www.bookgarden.com
www.csustan.edu
www.ipl.org
www.yarmouthport.com
www.factmonster.com
www.bournehistoricalsoc.org
www.mayflowerfamiles.com
www.ida.net
www.uwm.edu
www.magma.ca
www.micsem.org
www.barnstablecountyfair.org
www.adb.online.anu.edu.au/biogs/
http://noviomagus.tripod.com
http://uk.music.yahoo.com
virtualclassroom.org
encarta.msn.com
slate.msn.com/id/91350

Other Sources:
Records of The Harwich Temperance Reform Club, 1874, Cape Cod Community College.
Story from Jay Crowell about his parents, Joshua and Elinor Crowell of Dennis.
Letter from Donald R. Abbott, USAF Texas Towers Association
Playhouse Playbill, August 7, 1939
Playhouse Playbill, August 14, 1939
Epoch Retirement Center, 2002, Mrs. Kathleen McDonough
Falmouth Historical Society collection
Dictionary of American Biography, Volume 8, page 539. New York, NY: Charles Scribner.
The Descendants of Richard Knowles, 1637-1973, page 281
Will of Joseph Rogers
Barnstable Directory of 1895
Ships' Figureheads of Old Cape Cod. Hyannis, MA: Cape Cod Advancement Plan, 1936.
Cape Cod Community College, West Barnstable, MA. William Brewster Nickerson Room, archives collection: letter/journal of Albert Smith describing a trip by packet from Boston to Orleans in 1847.
Copy of letter donated by Stanley W. Smith
Walter Babbitt Collection: William Brewster Nickerson Room, Cape Cod Community College, West Barnstable, MA. Original letter on file.
The Thomas Clark Family: Genealogy of the Descendents of Thomas Clark of Plymouth, 1623, by Arthur Radasch, 1972. Sturgis Public Library.

Elmer Landers letter to Alice Gibbs, Bourne Archives, Bourne, MA

Burgess Genealogy, pages 390-394.

The S Boats: Gallant Ladies of the Past, by Richard A. Tucker, Internet

Collection of Starling Burgess's papers at the G.W. Blunt Library at Mystic Seaport in Connecticut.

Brewster Vital Records. Published by the Massachusetts Society of Mayflower Descendants, Boston, MA., 1904.

Memoirs of Alfred Ristieaux

Memoirs of Dr. F.J. McNulty Assistant Ship's Surgeon CSS Shenendoah

Gerard Ward: American Activities in the Central Pacific, 1967

Nickerson Family Genealogy, Volume IV. page 130.

Cape Cod Legends, a 1935 Hyannis pamphlet published by the "Cape Cod Advancement Plan."

The Baseball Encyclopedia. Published by MacMillan Publishing Co., 8th edition, New York, NY., 1990, page 2012.

"Why Woods Hole?" by James Watt Mavor, Jr.. Published in Spritsail, Woods Hole, MA., Vol. 12, No. 2, 1998, page 19.

Dennis Town Records, Book no. 3, pages 394 and 399.

"Glimpses" published by Christian History Institute, P.O. Box 540, Worcester, Pennsylvania. e-mail chglimpses@aol.com/internet reference.

The Captive in Patagonia, or Life Among the Giants, A personal narrative by Benjamin Franklin Bourne, published by Gould and Lincoln, Boston, 1853.

The History of Richard Bourne and Some of his Descendants, by Hannah S. B. Dykes pages 89-100.

U.S. Life Saving Service Report for 1886, Published by the Treasury Department, Washington DC., document 999, page 181, and U.S. Life Saving Service Report for 1887, published by the Treasury Department, Washington, DC. Document 1112, page 48,49.

Annual Report of the Operations of the United States Life Saving Service for 1894. U.S. Government Printing Office, Washington, DC. Document no. 1740, 1895. pages 39-44.

Personal papers provided to the author by Philip Ellis Chisholm, Great Great Grandson of Captain Sidney A. Ellis.

"Beachcombers, Traders, and Castaways in Micronesia," Website micsem.org

Photo Credit:

Front cover photo: *Harvesting Salt Hay on Barnstable's Great Marshes*. Source: *Population and Resources of Cape Cod: A Special Report in Recognition of the Three Hundredth Anniversary of the Settlement of New England.* Published by the Commonwealth of Massachusetts Department of Labor and Industries, Wright & Potter Printing Company, Boston, Massachusetts, 922, page 36.

Back cover photo by Adriana Sheedy.